Praise for *Thrive*

Lina is kind of like the feminine version of the apostle Paul—she's a straight-shooting, no-holds-barred, truth-slinging gospel warrior! I admire her passion for God, her knowledge of His Word, and her heart for His people, and all three of those characteristics are present from cover to cover of *Thrive*. This is one of the most practical, hopeful, Jesus-focused books I've ever read on the subject of singleness!

—**LISA HARPER**
Author, Bible teacher, and
Women of Faith *speaker*

Thrive is rivetingly raw and gloriously victorious . . . a goldmine for singles and marrieds alike!

—**LYNNE TELLSCHOW**
Director of Women's Ministry,
Harvest Bible Chapel, Elgin, Illinois

In a world full of families, singleness can be a major challenge. There have been lots of books and seminars aimed at helping singles cope and conquer, but often not backed up with the power and principles of God's Word. Thankfully, Lina has done just that in a book that is bound to live up to its title for those called to a life of singleness.

—**DR. JOSEPH M. STOWELL**
President, Cornerstone University,
Grand Rapids, Michigan

Thrive is, in a word, BOLD. Her fresh perspectives on singleness as a gift, temptations that most don't mention, the real tensions living in a world where matching means another person, set this book apart as not only a must read for singles, but a must study, dialogue, and debate book. Attitudes and obstacles are examined in the bright light of Scripture with the precision and focus of this emergency room doctor perspective that is uniquely Lina. Read and prepare for bold, biblical impact.

—**MIRIAM NEFF**
President of Widow Connection

Thrive:
The Single Life as God Intended

Lina AbuJamra

MOODY PUBLISHERS

CHICAGO

Edited by Bailey Utecht
Interior design: Ragont Design
Cover design: Maralynn Jacoby

Library of Congress Cataloging-in-Publication Data

AbuJamra, Lina.
Thrive : the single life as God intended / Lina AbuJamra.
    pages cm
ISBN 978-0-8024-0714-6
1. Single people--Religious life. I. Title.
BV4596.S5Z28 2013
248.8'4--dc23

2012047134

We hope you enjoy this book from Moody Publishers. Our goal is to provide high-quality, thought-provoking books and products that connect truth to your real needs and challenges. For more information on other books and products written and produced from a biblical perspective, go to www.moodypublishers.com or write to:

Moody Publishers
820 N. LaSalle Boulevard
Chicago, IL 60610

1 3 5 7 9 10 8 6 4 2

Printed in the United States of America

To Milo and Fawzi—
they taught me how to thrive,
and I'm forever grateful.

Contents

Foreword

There is little real debate anymore about what the Bible means. Camps have formed, sides have been taken, and little if anything is freshly debated. Though we know what the Bible means, we desperately need flesh-and-blood examples of it lived. How can we take the authoritative message of God's Word and make it work in real life, dark culture, Western world reality? While the example of living the biblical mandates is needed in every societal strata and segment, it is needed most acutely where the challenges we face are greatest.

Given the sexually charged culture and the constant media pressure to "be in love," to "satisfy ourselves," to "do what feels best," I am constantly on the lookout for single adults who love Christ and are living His message in an exemplary way. Dr. Lina Abujamra is the example so many are searching for. An accomplished pediatrician, Lina has taken her medical experience to some of the toughest mission fields in the world and expressed the love of Christ to "the least of these." Today, Lina continues to practice pediatric emergency medicine even as she has assumed the role of director of women's ministry on the largest campus of Harvest Bible Chapel. Lina is an engaging and effective communicator of God's Word and has refused the traps so many unmarried Christians fall into. She has not put her life on hold nor has allowed impurity to become inevitable. She has courageously turned away from marriage opportunities that were not God's will for her life. She has insisted upon actually living the message of biblical and eternal priorities, and in the process has become one of the most dynamic and contagious Christians you will ever meet.

But she is not naive or content with easy answers either. Lina pulls no punches in *Thrive*. While Lina understands that "singleness" is not a disease for which marriage is the only cure, she refuses to placate or provide easy answers. She opens her Bible and with great candor brings God's Word to bear upon the Christian single adult experience in our culture. If you long to live victoriously regardless of your marital status, and if you want to get out of "limbo" and embrace with joy what God has for you right now, regardless of the future, you will be greatly helped by this book. If you are already in a relationship or married, this book will speak to you as it has to me. It will give you greater capacity to see and savor others regardless of their marital status and understand better how to minister to the "whole church."

If you're touchy and easily offended, put this book down now. But if you are ready for a real person, who is truly living a Christ-honoring life of singleness, and you can handle real candor about real struggles, a wonderful blessing is headed your way. Apply carefully the lessons of *Thrive* and your life in Christ will reach a new level of joy and victory.

Dr. James MacDonald
Senior Pastor, Harvest Bible Chapel (Greater Chicago area) and author of *Vertical Church, Lord Change Me,* and *Authentic*
Jamesmacdonald.com

Introduction:
You Were Made for More

If you're single, you're familiar with this scene.

It's a beautiful Sunday morning. The air is crisp, the sun bright. You're on time for a change. You smell good. You look good. Even your hair turned out great. You walk into the Sunday school room resplendent in fluorescent lighting, and do a 360, your version of Christian recon. You're new to the church, new to the singles group. You're ready for anything to happen. You're ready to meet "the one." But then you see it—the familiar box of Krispy Kremes, and you smell it, the aroma of badly singed coffee. In your peripheral vision, over in the far corner of the room, you spot the infamous huddle. You size each one of them up, while every head swivels your way, and several pairs of eyes zero in on you. Each of the young men silently scans you up and down, assessing you, carefully mulling you over. You see the internal debate as they study your face. Are you the one? Are you the answer to years of waiting and unspoken prayer requests?

Over on your right, you sense the regulars even before you see them—a group of single ladies also in their Sunday best—hoping the new face in the crowd, yours, hasn't dimmed their chances of catching "the one." They want to like you, they really do, but the jury is still out. You're still an unknown threat, and you did put on a a killer pair of shoes. You've got to make a decision, and you've got to make it fast. Do you walk over the cliff and into what is better known as the church singles scene, or do you turn and run? You hesitate for a split second, but suddenly the answer is as clear as the bright blue sky. This is not your scene. You do not belong here. Deep in your heart, you know you were made for more. Deep in your soul, you know that your life was meant to be about more than just hoping, looking, and waiting for "the one."

You were made to thrive.

Before you've had time to process this new revelation, you turn and run. And as you run, you catch your reflection in the window, and you notice something else: you're smiling.

It's been over ten years since I found myself at that very crossroad in that very same singles Sunday school class, and today I'm still smiling, though I'm no longer running.

By my midtwenties, I'd already read Joshua Harris's *I Kissed Dating Goodbye* and found it irrelevant to me as I hadn't even met my dating life yet. I'd also read *How to Know If Someone Is Worth Pursuing in Two Dates or Less* and knew I could one-up the author with my version of the book that I'd call *How to Know If Someone Is Worth Pursuing in Two Minutes or Less*. I knew enough by my midtwenties to know that if God's purpose for my life was simply to wait for Mr. Right to show up, then I was in for a long and boring life.

As a Christian woman, I'd been taught that Jesus had died for my sin and promised me abundant life. Surely Christ didn't sacrifice His life on the cross simply to land me in a room full of sticky donuts and stale coffee, waiting for the right man to find me? Surely God hadn't meant for my entire adult life to remain on hold until a guy sitting in a huddle somewhere mustered up the guts to finally make a move? Had God really saved me just to place me on some high-reaching shelf, waiting for the right man so my life could finally begin?

If you're reading this book, chances are you fall into one of three categories: (1) you're married and know the perfect single person to gift it to; (2) you're my mother (Mom, this is where I'm supposed to remind myself to make you promise to skip over chapter 3—it's the sex chapter); or (3) you're single and are sick and tired of yet another singles book on waiting. Perhaps you're hoping for a book on living. Perhaps you're looking for a book on thriving.

I'm glad you found this book.

This book is not a critique of church singles groups. For years, well-meaning churches have tried to minister to the growing segment of single evangelicals, hiring nice, young, good-looking married men with beautiful wives to lead the growing number of Christian singles in the United States. They preach sermons on how to get married, stay married, and have great marital sex, so long as purity is maintained during the interminable singles years. They make sure to throw in "I'm married to a beautiful woman and we have great sex together," every few minutes, as if to remind all the single ladies that the typical singles pastor is untouchable and already spoken for.

Meanwhile, the church remains full of single men and women who walk in and out of the doors of their potential mating soil. They pray that the windows of heaven would finally open, that God in His great mercy would finally take note of them and deliver them from the suffering of the single Christian life. They live in a society made for marriage, in churches geared for couples, in a world where twos rule. Week after week, they leave brokenhearted and confused, with a growing list of questions about God and His ways: Has God forgotten or overlooked the single Christian? Where is God in the single Christian life? Is it possible to thrive without a soul mate?

And the most sobering question of them all: Is this all there is? Is this the abundant life that I've been promised? Is this fullness of joy and pleasures forevermore or am I missing something?

If God's promises are true, then you were made to thrive no matter what your marital status is. If God's Word is true, then the waiting ended the moment you embraced Jesus Christ as your Lord and Savior. If God's Word is true, then you have everything you need for life and for godliness. You are not half of a whole; you were made whole in Christ. You are not part of an incomplete equation; the equation has already been resolved in Christ. You are not a mystery to be solved; Christ is the answer to every question you have ever asked and every puzzle you have ever agonized over.

You were made for more.

If God's primary will for men and women is to get married and have kids, then He's dropped the ball on 45 percent of the American people.[1] If God's primary will for mankind is for men and women to live in perfect wedded bliss, then He must have forgotten to give the memo to Jesus Christ. And if God's will for mankind is to find the big love and spend eternity with the wife of your youth, then the most confused person in the world is the apostle Paul in 1 Corinthians 7. But God didn't create you to just get married and bear kids. God hasn't saved you and put you on hold until your right partner comes around. God isn't holding His breath, wondering when you will get over your commitment phobia and get on with His will.

You were created to know God's love and be radically changed by it. You were made to love God with every ounce of your being. Christ died to turn your life upside down for His glory and the renown of His name.

You were made to thrive.

And it starts right now. No more waiting for Mr. Right. No more wondering if your train has passed you by. No more pondering what went wrong.

It's time for you to live the life that Christ rescued you for. It's time for you to thrive.

In the following pages, I'm going to show you from God's Word what it means to thrive, and how to live the life that thrives. We will discuss five attitudes that every single Christian must embrace in order to thrive. I'll also point out four obstacles that single Christians must overcome. Finally, we'll talk about how to actually make it happen.

This book is for every single Christian. It's a book about understanding what the life that thrives looks like and how to get there. If you're ready to move beyond the waiting and finally break free into the life that God has created you for, then this book is for you.

Thrive

MY SAD SINGLE STORY

I was born at five thirty in the morning on a glorious Saturday in April—which makes me thoughtful but not nice. A nice person would have waited until at least eight o'clock to come out, but a less thoughtful person would have made it through the tunnel at three o'clock in the morning instead. Little could I have predicted that the story of my birth would be a foreshadowing of my future dating life. I ended two engagements over a ten-year period of the best years of my life, proving once again that I'm thoughtful but not nice. I'm thoughtful because in both cases I saved my fiancés from a life of slow and painful torture, but definitely not nice, because a nice girl would have simply said no to a proposal of marriage in the first place.

Regardless, I've found myself back in the bull pen or the waiting room of life that every single Christian knows and dreads.

I suppose working as an ER doctor for the last fifteen years has made me a bit of an expert when it comes to waiting rooms. I can tell you that all kinds of crazy things happen in the waiting room. People bleed out in the waiting room. They talk, they fight, they eat, and they stare into space in the waiting room. Sometimes they even die in the waiting room.

But worst of all, people get forgotten in the waiting room.

It happened to me once. I was waiting for my turn to see the doctor when I had to step away to the ladies' room for a second. I debated the wisdom of going, but it was a matter of life and death, and the bladder has a way of trumping everything else. I made the agonizing decision to go.

I was gone three minutes, tops, but it was long enough—

long enough to blink, long enough to get passed by. Next thing you know, it's too late. Your name has been called out, and you're officially put in the leftover bin. You're lucky if your name ever gets called out again. So you go on waiting until God knows when. And I suppose I'm still waiting.

That's my sad single story.

I never planned on being single at forty. No one plans on that. I'm pretty sure I've never met anyone who grew up dreaming of living happily ever after—alone. I don't remember ever seeing a movie or reading a book where the star thought to herself, *When I grow up, I can't wait to go on vacation alone*; or *Oh boy, someday, when I finally can, I'll get all dressed up and head out to dinner at a fancy restaurant—on my own.*

Yet here I am—forty and single, thoughtful but not nice, and still waiting.

Or am I?

A few years ago, I went into a restaurant and gave my name to the hostess. After writing it down, the lady gave me a funny-looking square to hold on to.

"Keep this with you," she said. "It will buzz when your name is called out."

And in that instant, in the blink of an eye, my life was radically changed. Armed with the magic square in my hand, I was given the freedom to enjoy the beauty of life in the waiting room. There were places I could go, vending machines I could explore. There were cafeterias to be visited and people to get to know.

The waiting room had metamorphosed into a place of thriving, a place where dreams could be born and life could be lived. The waiting room had suddenly become a gift.

IT'S A WONDERFUL LIFE

If you stop and think about the singles in the Bible, you won't find that many of them. Ruth was single until she met Boaz. Esther was single until someone discovered her hidden potential and turned her into a beauty queen (I guess you can thank God for every Disney movie ever made since Esther). Abigail became single for about a day after Naboth died until David heard about it and asked for her hand in marriage. Then there was my favorite single virgin in the Bible, the daughter of Jephthah in Judges 11 who was banished to a life of permanent virginity because of her father's rash vow.

The New Testament list is even shorter. Perhaps it's because after Christ's death and resurrection, the context of relationship changed. No longer is your blood family your primary family. When you became born again and began walking in Jesus Christ, the context for your relationships shifted from the family you were born into to your church family, the bride of Christ.

The apostle Paul, arguably the greatest Christian of all time, understood relationships even better than Dr. Phil does. Paul himself remained single and spent much of his time writing about relationships and how to grow, despite the difficult ones. In this book, we'll be spending some time in 1 Corinthians 7. If you're familiar with the Bible, then you know that 1 Corinthians 7 is the singles, sex, and marriage chapter.

Interestingly, in 1 Corinthians 7 Paul doesn't refer to singleness as the resigned lot of those who aren't wily enough to find a partner. He doesn't describe singleness as a curse or a punishment or even a temporary state of waiting until the right man comes along. Quite the contrary. Paul is convinced throughout 1 Corinthians 7 of the blessing of the single life. Throughout the chapter, he uses three key ideas to describe the blessings of singleness, proving that singleness is indeed a place you can thrive in. Let me show you what Paul thought.

IT'S A GOOD LIFE

The single life is a good life. When God created the world in Genesis 1, He looked at each day He created and said that it was good. It was well done. It was perfect. The word *good* is a good word. I'm not much of a cook, but I appreciate good food. When I taste something good, not only am I pleased with it in the moment, but I look forward to tasting it again—the sooner the better! When I see a good movie, chances are I'll want to rent it or buy it for myself.

Good is good.

So when Paul describes the single life in 1 Corinthians 7:8, it's fitting that he uses the word *good*. Here's what he says: "To the unmarried and the widows I say that *it is good for them to remain single* as I am."

The single life is a good life. No more wondering if God has given you second best. No more asking why everyone has been more blessed by God while you keep on waiting. No more misinterpreting God's Word and His ways.

You have been given a good life. Is it permanent? Is it irrevocable? Are you doomed to a life of eternal virginity and aloneness? As you flip the pages of this book, I hope to answer every one of your questions. For now, settle it in your mind that God is big enough and wise enough to give you the best life possible—the life that thrives.

So stop wasting it. Stop wishing it away. Stop complaining

about it and praying that it would change soon, and start believing the truth of God's Word.

You have been given a good life, and it's yours by design. Do you believe it?

IT'S A PURPOSE-DRIVEN LIFE

Not only is the single life a good life, but according to Paul in 1 Corinthians 7, it is a life of purpose. Do you ever wonder what God wants you to do with your single life? Do you ever wonder what your purpose is as a single Christian without a husband to care for or kids to nurture?

Stop wondering and listen to Paul's words in 1 Corinthians 7:32: "I want you to be free from anxieties. *The unmarried man is anxious* about the things of the Lord, *how to please the Lord.*"

I hope you pick up on what Paul is saying. Your purpose in life is to please the Lord. Your life will thrive when you become obsessed with pleasing the Lord. Later on in the book, we'll further explore the meaning of this freedom that Paul alludes to and how every single Christian can take full advantage of it. We'll also talk about undivided devotion to God and how to get it.

But for now, suffice it to say that your purpose as a single Christian is to please the Lord. You cannot please the Lord when you're nursing a grudge about your singleness. You cannot please the Lord when you're questioning His judgment and criticizing His will. You cannot please the Lord when you place your desires higher than His purposes for your life.

Your purpose in life has not been botched by your singleness. You are not a mutant in God's design for marriage.

God created you for the sole purpose of knowing Him and making Him known. Your singleness is God's perfect place for you to thrive. You don't have to wait for your knight in shining armor to start living. You can know the Lord fully and serve Him wholly right here, right now.

What you've forgotten is that you do have a knight, but He didn't come on a horse. He was born in a stable. He developed calluses on His hands, and died on a cross to call you His own. You were created to know Him and make Him known.

Are you living out God's purpose for your life?

IT'S A HAPPIER LIFE

Good is good, and having purpose is good, but sometimes good is just not good enough. I'm not a fan of average. I like chocolate, but I much prefer a chocolate explosion dessert. And I like strawberries, but give me a chocolate-covered strawberry anytime.

I may settle for good, but I'm looking for great.

To call the single Christian life a good life is a place to start, but this book isn't about settling for good. It's about looking for great. It's a book about thriving. When I think about thriving, I can't help but picture a lush green tree with plenty of fruit for picking. Or I picture a wound that's healing well with plenty of granulation tissue and healthy pink, blood-tinged skin forming around the edges. Okay, that was unnecessary, but you get the point.

Paul, of all people, understood the tension that single Christians face. And if you know anything about Paul, he was not a man who settled for average. The guy was passionate, full-throttle, all the way. So Paul finishes his thesis on singleness in 1 Corinthians 7:40 with just one more little nugget—one more blessing not to be overlooked.

Yes, singleness is good. And yes, the single life has purpose. But now Paul makes one more astounding statement. Here's what he says: "Yet in my judgment *she [the unmarried] is happier if she remains as she is.* And I think that I too have the Spirit of God."

Did you catch it? I can hardly believe it. Every time I read this verse, my jaw hits the floor. I know that theologians argue about whether verse 40 was divinely inspired or simply Paul's words, but I'll take Paul's words over my own opinion on any given day. I also believe that God has allowed this verse to remain in His Word specifically to encourage every single Christian who is convinced that true joy is beyond grasp. It's not! Paul, in this unbelievably bold verse, settles every question about singleness you may ever have.

Life is happier as a single follower of Jesus Christ.

I can already see you putting words in my mouth. I'm not attacking marriage. I believe that God loves marriage and uses it as the primary example of the union between Christ and His bride, the church. But I cannot read Paul's words in 1 Corinthians 7:40 and not come to the simple conclusion that the single Christian life is a happier life.

The most obvious question that comes to my mind then is this: *If the single Christian life is happier, why don't more single Christians feel happy?*

Many reasons come to mind. It could be because single Christians have embraced the lies of our culture and society about love and sex. It could be because of a lack of knowing and believing God's Word. Or maybe your story is much more painful than I can ever imagine.

Here's what I do know: God's Word is alive and active, and God uses it to help you discern the truth about your heart. So as you turn the pages of this book, I pray that God will reveal Himself to you in your point of pain. I pray that the Spirit of God will convict you where you need to change, and I pray that God will help you overcome in the areas where you need victory.

My prayer for you is not only to understand what it means to thrive, but to know how to live the life that thrives, and then, by the grace and strength of God, to do it.

If you're ready for it, go ahead. Turn the page.

PART 1

The Gift of Singleness

1

No Exchanges, No Returns: The Gift of Singleness

It's Christmas morning. Everyone in the family can't wait to open their presents. There's cheering and there's laughing until my turn comes. I can feel every eye on me. I need a moment of privacy. It happens every Christmas, and I know it's going to happen again. I'm going to get another gift I absolutely can't stand. This time, I refuse to let my expression be captured on video. I refuse to make my gift-loathing known for generations to come. I will win the battle of the undesirable gift and learn to receive it with grace.

Ask anyone in my family. I'm the worst person in the world to buy gifts for. I never know what I want, and no matter what I get, I typically hate it.

If you're single, you know exactly what I mean when I start talking about unwanted and undesirable gifts. Every single Christian has had to sit through a conversation that sounds a little bit like this:

"So, tell me, are you dating anyone?"

"Nope. I'm not," you answer quickly, hoping to get the conversation over with.

"Really. How old are you now? Shouldn't you be settling down by now?" the questioner persists, oblivious to the hideous nature of the question.

"I don't know," you mumble. "I mean, I know I'm getting older, but I seem to be doing okay."

"Oh. I see. You have the gift of singleness. That's it, isn't it?"

While I'm sure that most people really mean well when they grant you the gift of singleness in a sentence, I can assure you that nothing bothers the single Christian more than the assumption that God has given you this "special" gift of singleness. Singleness, a gift? Where in the world would anyone come up with such a grotesque idea? And if singleness is a gift, can someone please point me to the return counter?

IF SINGLENESS is a gift, can someone please point me to the return counter?

Further inquiry into the idea of singleness as a gift reveals that it was not an idea made up by your great-aunt Midge, but by none other than the apostle Paul in his letter to the Corinthian church. I've already alluded to the passage in the introduction, but over the course of this book, we're going to spend a big portion of our time in 1 Corinthians 7, so you may as well go ahead and get familiar with its content right now. It's Paul's treatise on singleness and marriage.

But let me start by giving you a little background on the church in Corinth.

THE CHURCH IN CORINTH

In Paul's day, Corinth was the most important city in all of Greece. It was wealthy. It was luxurious. And it was chock-full of immorality. The people of Corinth spent their days attending tournaments and speeches. In other words, they loved sports and politics. Sounds familiar, doesn't it? They liked to have fun much like most Americans do in our modern-day world.

Enter Paul.

In Acts 18, we're given the account of how the gospel reached the people of Corinth. It was during Paul's second missionary journey that it happened. He was about fifty years old at the time and single, a tentmaker by trade. As soon as he got to Corinth he met a nice couple, Priscilla and Aquila, also tentmakers, and the three of them set up shop. Paul spent a year and a half in Corinth, making tents by day and preaching the gospel by night. By the time Paul was ready to move on, a church had been birthed.

Sadly, the church in Corinth had no sooner taken off than it started sputtering along without the strong leadership of Paul. Unable to break from the carnality of the culture, the worldliness of the city soon infected the fellowship of believers. Cliques were formed. Lawsuits started flying around between believers. Women abandoned modesty. Arguments broke out over marriage, spiritual gifts, and life as a follower of Jesus Christ.

The church, unsure of what to do, wrote to the apostle Paul and asked for advice. Paul was on his third missionary journey by now, and while in Ephesus, he sat down and wrote the two letters to the church in Corinth known to us today as First and Second Corinthians.

The first letter to the Corinthian church began with Paul's usual greeting, but Paul then quickly narrowed in on the heart of the matter. He was quick to warn the church that its greatest danger came not from the outside, but from within, in the form of divisions and cliques in the church (1 Corinthians 1:11). He reminded the church that its only leader and center ought to be Christ. Apart from His leadership, there would be no church. Paul reminded the Corinthian church of the meaning of salvation and reviewed the basics of the gospel on which everything else in the Christian life hinges.

By the time Paul reached chapter 5, he was ready to discuss in greater detail the specific point of immorality that was going on in the Corinthian church: a man was having an incestuous affair with his stepmother. That's bad no matter how you look at it. Paul admonished the church to clean things up and refused to condone this man's sinful behavior. Paul wrote one of the strongest passages on immorality in the Bible in 1 Corinthians 6:9–20. Paul then drove home the point that in Christ, our bodies are not our own. God owns us. He paid for us with a price—the precious blood of Jesus Christ, God's own Son. Because we've been purchased by Christ's death, we can no longer live as we choose. We must now live as God desires, no matter the context of our closest relationships, single or married.

To further expound on how the Christian life ought to look, Paul moved into 1 Corinthians 7 and broke down the who/what/when/where/why of marriage and singleness.

By now you have a clearer picture of the culture in which

1 Corinthians was written. It was a culture of moral decay and corruption. It was a culture that was affecting the church in Corinth. It was a culture very much like our own.

Have you ever wondered whether God understands the stress and temptation that single Christians face today? Have you ever wondered if you as a single Christian immersed in a culture of great sensuality can live a holy life that thrives? The answer is a resounding yes. Just ask Paul as we embark on his teachings on singleness and sex to a church caught in the midst of a morally corrupt world and culture.

But I digress. We'll talk about sex and singleness later on in the book. Right now I'd like to introduce you to the concept of singleness as the gift that God has lovingly and purposefully given you in order to thrive.

SINGLENESS AS A GIFT

I once wanted a blender for Christmas really, really badly. Every time I came across a recipe, even though I don't cook, I seemed to think that it absolutely needed this particular stainless steel and glass blender. Every time I felt thirsty, I dreamed of the wonderful drinks I could make with that specific blender. So I did what every smart woman would do: I made sure I told the right people what I wanted, and when Christmas morning finally came around, I acted delighted and appropriately surprised when I unwrapped the package and saw the beautiful blender that was everything I thought it would be and more. My dream had come true.

Two years have gone by since I received that perfect gift, and I'd like you to take a moment and try to guess how many times I've used my blender so far. Go ahead. Write it down.

31

Are you ready for the answer? If you guessed twice, you are correct.

Now allow me to tell you about another Christmas gift on a different Christmas. It was finally my turn to open my present. I held the package and wondered what could be so big and so fluffy. I hadn't asked for anything that year, and certainly for nothing so big and quite so fluffy. I tentatively opened the package, carefully watching my facial expressions. By the time I processed that what I held in my hands was a big and fluffy red blanket, it was too late to hide my dismay. A blanket for Christmas? Who would give such a— how can I say this politely—*useful* gift to anyone? I took my blanket home with no plans to use it and started making up a list of folks I could regift it to.

Little did I know that the red blanket would become a family and personal favorite, and the saving grace to my very cold basement for years to come. I can't keep track of the friends who have snuggled beneath its warmth and wondered as to its softness. The blanket that I would have never chosen turned out to be this girl's best friend and the best Christmas gift I have ever received.

It's a funny thing about gifts. The gift you think you can't live without ends up sitting unused on a shelf somewhere in your home, while the gift you initially can't stand turns out to be the one item you can't live without.

The truth is that, most of the time, you and I have very little concept as to what we truly need in our lives. Our desires are affected by what we see on television, what advertisers tell us we need, or by what our friends have. Our wants are often molded by our backgrounds, upbringing, and culture. They are influenced by the last movie we watched or the latest book we read. Most of us give only a passing regard to what God deeply desires for our lives.

It shouldn't surprise us then that we apply the same rules when it comes to our singleness.

Singleness, a gift? The very idea is appalling. Who would ever give anyone such a—how can I say it politely—*useless* gift? Weren't we made for marriage and sex and kids and car seats?

If you're single, you know exactly what I'm talking about. Singleness is the gift that you never wanted, never planned on, and wish you'd never opened. Surely there's been a mistake. Surely this is not your gift to keep forever and happily ever after?

But a careful look at God's Word reveals that your gift is no mistake. We've been talking about 1 Corinthians 7, and if you'll read verse 7 you'll see that it was Paul who brought up the concept of singleness as a gift. Here is what he says in 1 Corinthians 7:7: "I wish that all were as I myself am. *But each has his own gift from God*, one of one kind and one of another."

YOU AND I have very little concept as to what we truly need in our lives.

Wait—say that again? Singleness—a gift? Why in the world would anyone consider singleness a gift? It sounds more like a curse to most people. And if it is a gift, who is "lucky" enough to have it? Or if I may make it even more personal: Do you have the gift of singleness?

I believe the best way to answer this question is to consider some basic characteristics of this so-called gift.

CHARACTERISTICS OF THE GIFT

When discussing the gift of singleness, there are three characteristics of the gift that you must observe from 1 Corinthians 7:7.

First, it is a personal gift. The word *each* insinuates the idea that this gift is personal. God gives each person a gift. It is the perfect gift because it's given personally to each individual with great thought and care.

Second, it is a unique gift. To further emphasize his point, Paul reminds us that this isn't a grab bag, white elephant gift exchange. The Word of God says that each person has his own gift. This gift has been uniquely given to each person by the Lord. It is a unique gift.

Third, it is a gift from God. The most amazing thing about this gift of singleness isn't just that it was designed specifically with you in mind, but that the giver of the gift is God Himself. He fashioned the gift. He made it perfectly and uniquely and personally for you. God gave you the best gift possible, knowing everything there is to know about you and your life. That's pretty amazing.

Your gift is not an accident. It's not a mistake. It's not a joke. It is for real. It doesn't get much better than that!

You may be thinking to yourself, *But that doesn't seem fair. Why in the world would God give me the gift of single-*

ness? Doesn't He know me at all? Or you may be thinking, *What if I don't want this gift? Can I return it? Is it too late to exchange it?*

These are great questions, and by the time you finish this book, I hope you will have the answers you're looking for. For now, let's consider the gift of singleness from God's perspective. Is the gift of singleness yours permanently, or only for a season? And do you have any choice in the matter of your giftedness?

SINGLE BY GIFTING

So far in my life, I've met two people who believe they actually have the spiritual gift of singleness. In other words, they genuinely believe that God has called them to be single for the rest of their lives and have no desire to ever be married. I cynically glaze over when they start talking, because deep down, I believe that they are likely to change their minds if the right six-foot tall, dark-haired, blue-eyed, washboard ab'ed guy showed up at their doorstep.

Maybe you're not as cynical as I am, but the truth is that only a small number of people reading this book believe that the gift of singleness is the most natural and desirable gift ever given to them by God.

The "single-by-gifting" Christian makes me think of Matthew 19:12. In this passage, Jesus is having a very interesting conversation with the people about divorce. The disciples, puzzled over Jesus' statement about divorce, make the conclusion that people would be better off remaining single. To that, Jesus acknowledges that indeed some people have been given the gift of singleness and as such, are very happy to remain single, and thus avoid divorce. Look at Jesus' words in Matthew 19:12: "For there are eunuchs who have been so from birth, and there are eunuchs who have been made eunuchs by men, and there are eunuchs who have made themselves eunuchs for the sake of the kingdom of heaven. Let the one who is able to receive this receive it."

You probably haven't used the word *eunuch* in a conversation today, so I looked it up for you. According to Wikipedia, a eunuch is a person who may have been castrated and who often worked as a harem guard or palace official. Wikipedia goes on to say that according to ancient texts, a eunuch may also refer to a man who is not castrated but who is impotent, celibate, or otherwise not inclined to marry and reproduce.[2] Regardless of Wikipedia's definition, Christ used the term, not in a derogatory fashion, but in quite a positive way.

What Jesus was saying is that a single-by-gifting person is like the eunuch whose sexual urges do not control him and who is happy to remain single.

If you're reading this and realize that you fit the description of single by gifting—good for you. You're probably the exception to the rule in our sexually charged culture, and you can consider yourself blessed. You're happily single by gifting, and nothing would push you over to the other side.

Before you close this book and figure you're good to go, let me warn you that just because you're single by gifting doesn't mean that your life is necessarily thriving for the Lord. If you have the gift of singleness, the challenge for you is to think carefully about why God has given you this gift and how you will use it for His kingdom-building purposes.

So resist the urge to stop reading and make sure you finish the book.

SINGLE BY YOUR CHOOSING

The second category of the gift of singleness is the "single by your choosing" group. You fall in this group if you're one of those "who have made themselves eunuchs for the sake of the kingdom of heaven" (Matthew 19:12). I remember reading the story of Jim and Elisabeth Elliot. They had dated for a while and felt that they had found their soul mate in each other. However, Jim Elliot had other plans. He felt called to be a missionary to the Auca Indians. Elisabeth did not. So Jim became a eunuch for the sake of the kingdom of God. He ended his relationship with Elisabeth with no hopes of ever marrying the love of his life. He was determined not to let anything stand in the way of God's call for his life. Eventually God did change both Jim and Elisabeth's plans and they did get married, but not until both of them had fully surrendered their dreams of love and marriage to the Lord.

I've always been inspired by this love story because it clearly places love for God above love for another human being. We live in a culture that idolizes the "big love" so much so that it's hard for most of us to understand how anyone can choose anything over true love. Yet over the course of history, countless Christians have put their hands to the plow of serving the Lord and have never looked back, considering the reproach of Christ of far greater worth than the fleeting pleasures of what this life has to offer for a season. It sounds radical. It is. These Christians serve as an example for us today, and understood that the life that thrives is the life that dies to self and is fully surrendered to the Lord.

Of course the best example of a man who had the gift of singleness by his choosing is the apostle Paul. Paul understood that to serve God alone without the burden of a wife would benefit the kingdom of God far more than a life of temporary wedded bliss. Having been greatly influenced by this apostle's example, it's hard for me to disagree with his choice.

WE LIVE IN a culture that idolizes the "big love" so much so that it's hard for most of us to understand how anyone can choose anything over true love.

While you may not be single by gifting, if you've chosen a life of singleness to further build the kingdom of God, you will be greatly blessed and rewarded for it in due time. Paul commends this life of sacrifice and reminds us that the Lord is pleased with it.

As you read this book, I hope you will find it a blessing and an encouragement to you. You will likely face certain obstacles along the way of the single Christian life, and I hope this book will help you to overcome them as you grow closer to Jesus Christ.

SINGLE BY GOD'S CHOOSING

I'd venture to guess that most single Christians in today's culture fall into this category of singleness. Growing up, the last thing you had on your agenda was a life of barren singleness. You are not single by gifting. You are not single by your choosing as evidenced by the hundreds of dollars you've already spent on Internet dating subscriptions. No. You are single by God's choosing.

Drum roll please.

God has decided that, for better or for worse, the best gift for you right now is the gift of singleness.

I'm not sure how long you'll be stuck with this gift. I'm not sure why you've been given this gift. But until the Lord says so, you would do well to graciously accept His gift for you.

But I have another angle for you to consider.

Could it be that God has given you this gift of singleness to deepen your walk with Him? Could it be that God wants to use your unfulfilled longings to draw you closer to Himself? In other words, could there be a purpose to this gift that God has given you?

I know what you're thinking. *Why me? Why do I have to learn this way while everyone else I know can learn the same lessons within the confines of a biblical marriage? Is it something I've done? Is it the way that I look? Was it something I said? Why would God choose me to carry this burden?*

I believe that you will find answers to these questions as you turn the pages of this book. I never planned on being single at forty. I thought I'd lived right and prayed right, and by God's grace, things would turn out right for me.

Little did I know that what our culture says is right is

often far different than what God considers right for His children. Little did I know that the road toward God is filled with valleys so deep and mountains so high that only His grace could sustain us through them.

GROWING UP, the last thing you had on your agenda was a life of barren singleness.

Here's a little known secret: you can embrace God's will for your life and thrive in it, even when it's not what you would have chosen for yourself in the first place, because God's gifts are the ones you never knew you needed but end up not being able to live without.

So how do you move from accepting a gift you may not have wanted to actually loving and enjoying it? How do you thrive when you feel like you've been given plan B? It starts by understanding who you are and what you've been given.

WHO AM I?

It happened shortly after I ended my engagement. I went home for the holidays and was getting a mani/pedi with my mother. Halfway through the job, the nice lady doing my nails and listening to my sad tale of disrupted love looked up, stared me in the eye, and with her broken English said this: "You lesbian?"

Despite all of our modern technology and advancements, we're still living in a culture that misunderstands the why of singleness. If you're over thirty and you're still single, the gay community will push you to admit who you really are. Feminists will commend you for standing up for who you are. Traditionalists will wonder where your parents went wrong. Society will tell you that you can still do something about it and change it. And the church simply doesn't know what to do with you.

In a culture where everything promotes marriage and family, the idea that anyone would be single by choice or giftedness seems preposterous. If you're single, there must be a reason. There must be something wrong with you. There must be a good explanation. Every other explanation for your singleness is too outrageous to validate.

The single Christian simply won't fit into a clean category. It used to be that if you passed age thirty and remained single, then you liked cats and still lived with your mother. Today's single Christian is a far cry from a cat-owning old maid—not that I have anything against cats.

Ironically, despite the freedoms and opportunities that most single Christians have in today's society, deep down you still wonder if there may be something wrong with you. You feel insignificant. You aren't sure where you fit in. You wonder who you really are.

Though the search for significance is not restricted to the single Christian, it certainly has a way of isolating the single Christian, leaving you with the impression that you're not sexy enough, you're not woman enough, or you're not good enough. Otherwise you'd be married by now.

Your sense of insignificance and confused identity is

propagated by the many social media outlets that remind you that everyone else in the world has figured it out, leaving you alone, isolated, needy, and unable to enjoy the gift that God has so graciously given you for this season of your life.

The worst part about it is that you know better. You know you shouldn't care what other people think. You know that you're not a lesbian, and that you're not a feminist. You know that you're smarter than that. But in the quiet of your soul, you find yourself wondering where your plus-one is.

IT USED TO be that if you passed age thirty and remained single, then you liked cats and still lived with your mother.

If you long for a life that thrives, you must accept the gift that's been given to you by God and embrace your true identity in Christ. Stop listening to the voice of the culture. Stop listening to your feelings. Stop dreaming of the life you think you ought to be living.

It's time to let go of the lies and embrace the truth of who you are in Christ.

YOU ARE NOT A SLOPPY LEFTOVER

I'm not a fan of leftovers. I'm too cheap not to take a doggie bag home from most restaurants, but anyone who knows me will tell you exactly what's going to happen to my bag of leftovers two days later. Yes—that bag of leftovers is going in the trash.

Whether you're a "never married but want to," or a "once married and hope to again," chances are you're familiar with sloppy leftovers. You know the gig. The good ones are married. The available ones are single for a reason. It's easy to feel like God's forgotten you and that you're nothing but a bag of leftovers. The idea of singleness as a God-given gift is preposterous. You tell yourself in your darker moments that if you wait long enough and pray desperately enough, someone's significant other will die and you will finally get your happy ending.

Allow me to introduce you to Hagar. Twice in Genesis she found herself in the wilderness, alone, afraid, and wondering what went wrong in her life. It wasn't Hagar's fault that she ended up pregnant. She was powerless to change the outcome dictated by her master Abraham. She only did what Sarah told her to do and ended up pregnant. Without much more than a second glance, Hagar is thrown out to the desert, treated like nothing more than a bag of trash.

It's a painful story, and I've always felt sorry for Hagar. She didn't deserve what happened to her. If anyone was a victim, it was Hagar. But she was anything but forgotten. With steadfast love and everlasting faithfulness, God saw value in Hagar and her unborn son. In Genesis 16, God reached down to Hagar in love and Hagar got the message. She called the Lord "the God who sees" in sure indication of her faith in a loving God.

If you're single and feel like you've been overlooked by

God, think again. God sees you and knows you. His gift to you is personal and intentional.

YOU ARE NOT PLAN B

I was never one of those girls who grew up dreaming about whether my bridesmaids would wear teal or organza, but I suppose just like everybody else, I assumed I'd get married, if not by my thirtieth birthday, then certainly by my thirty-fifth.

When what is expected, predicted, and seemingly God's will for all people doesn't happen to you, it's easy to wonder where things went wrong and what you could have done to change the outcome.

There was a guy who asked me out during medical school. To say that I hadn't dated much is an understatement. This was my first date ever. The guy was good-looking and polite. He was educated and had great table manners. His only fault was that he left me a bag of cookies on my doorstep after our second date. Many of you are swooning right now, but for me, nothing could have been worse. Maybe it was my own cultural traditions, or my fear of commitment, but all I could do was run in the other direction. Though I'm smart enough to understand that the odds of me marrying that guy back then were nil to nothing, there is hardly a year that goes by when I'm not tempted to wonder whether I'm living out God's plan B for my life because of my disdain for a dozen chocolate chip cookies.

It sounds ridiculous, but unfortunately many single Christians have believed similar lies when it comes to their singleness. Maybe you're one of them. Instead of trusting

God's wisdom in giving you the gift of singleness, you spend hours mulling over bad decisions you've made that have landed you in plan B of your Christian life.

NOTHING THAT happens in your life is outside of the will of God.

Read the next phrase and read carefully. Underline it if you must.

God makes no mistakes. You are not living plan B. Nothing that happens in your life is outside of the will of God. Your dating life is not God's big "oops." Your single life is not plan B. It's God's best for you. I believe with all of my heart that God, in His sovereignty, has allowed you to be single today for a reason, and that it is His plan not only to intentionally give you the gift of singleness but to also teach you how to thrive in it. Until you start believing God's truth in your life, you will not thrive.

This seems like a great place to remind you of who you are in Christ.

THIS IS WHO YOU ARE IN CHRIST

Whenever I'm trying to buy a gift for someone, one of the first things I do is think about that person. Who am I buying the gift for? What are they like? What do they like? The best gifts I've given are the ones where I really know the person I'm buying a gift for. I bet you've had the same experience.

Now think about God giving you the gift of singleness. No one knows you better than God does. In choosing your gift, He knows exactly what you like, who you are, and what will make you utterly, undeniably happy. I believe a review of who you are in Christ will help you to better accept the gift of singleness that God has given you.

YOU ARE CREATED

Do you ever look at yourself in the mirror and isolate the one thing about yourself that you can't stand? It may be your weight, or your nose, or your skin, but whatever it is, you convince yourself that your singleness is due to this one horrific feature of yours. One of the greatest battles that you will face as a single Christian is the idea that you are single because you haven't made the cut physically. If the marriage ship has passed you by, it's easy to stare at yourself in the mirror and blame your love handles, or your uneven skin, or your stubby fingers for your singleness. The truth is much harder to buy. You were created in God's image. He made you just the way you are. Your face is not an accident. Psalm 139:14 says, "I praise you, for I am fearfully and wonderfully made. Wonderful are your works; my soul knows it very well."

God's Word is amazing. Though the loudest voice in your head seems to be telling you that you're not pretty enough or perfect enough, there is another voice, a softer voice that tells you who you really are. It's a voice that reminds you that you're more than your face, your skin, your weight. It's a voice that whispers, "You were intricately woven by God in the depths of the earth." In other words, you are wonderful. You are beautiful. You were created in God's image. You are exactly who He created you to be.

The more you listen to that voice, the louder it will get. You were created by God to thrive.

YOU ARE CHOSEN

Not only are you created, but you are also chosen by God. It says in Psalm 139:16 that "your eyes saw my unformed substance . . . when as yet there was none of them." God saw you even before you were born. He knew what your face would look like and what kind of personality you'd have. He chose you, beloved.

In Ephesians 1:4–6 we're told that "even as he chose us in him before the foundation of the world, that we should be holy and blameless before him. In love he predestined us for adoption as sons through Jesus Christ, according to the purpose of his will, to the praise of his glorious grace, with which he has blessed us in the Beloved."

Remember when you were in grade school and had to pick dodgeball teams? My heart rate always went up. My palms started to sweat. Would anyone choose me? The waiting seemed to last forever.

If you're a single Christian whose time seems to have passed, whose marriage age seems to have come and gone, you may feel like the guy on the team who was never picked by anyone. It's easy to wonder what went wrong with you. You're believing a lie. No more lies. No more nonsense. It's time to live in the truth of God's Word. You were chosen by God before the foundation of the world.

You were chosen by Him to thrive.

YOU ARE GOD'S CHILD

My favorite story growing up was a book called *Are You My Mother?* It was the story of a bird whose mother went to find some worms. While she was gone, the bird panicked and got lost. The entire book is the story of the poor little bird walking around (because he hadn't learned how to fly yet) trying to find his lost mother. He runs into a cat and a truck and all kinds of things that don't look a thing like him. The poor little bird is on the verge of giving up hope of ever finding his mother, when she finally comes back. With one look at her, the little bird knows exactly who his mother is because he looks just like her.

I remember, even as a child, sensing the peace of belonging at the end of that little story. If you're a single Christian living in today's world, it's easy to feel like you don't belong. Even at church, with its good intentions, you may be tempted to feel like you don't belong.

WITH ONE LOOK at her, the little bird knows exactly who his mother is because he looks just like her.

The reason you feel like you don't belong is that you're not looking at your Father. Just like the little bird, you may be desperately looking for home, but you won't find it until you look at the face of Jesus Christ. You were not simply created to belong to a church scene or a social circle. You were made to belong in God's family as His child through His Son, Jesus Christ. You will only find true peace when you finally look at the face of your Father and see the obvious resemblance.

THE GREATEST GIFT OF ALL

The greatest gift you'll ever be given is the gift of Jesus Christ, God's Son. In Ephesians 2:8–9 here's how God says it: "For by grace you have been saved through faith. And this is not your own doing; it is the gift of God, not a result of works, so that no one may boast."

You cannot receive the gift of singleness until you find your likeness in God the Father by accepting the gift of His Son, Jesus Christ.

You may be even more familiar with John 3:16 that says this: "For God so loved the world, that he gave his only Son, that whoever believes in him should not perish but have eternal life."

When you're given a gift, it's not yours until you receive it. Whether we're talking about the gift of God's Son or your gift of singleness, there comes a point in time where you must take a step of faith and receive the gift you've been given.

It is when you receive the gift that you begin to thrive. And as great as the gift of singleness may be, it pales in comparison to the gift of God's Son.

I guess the ball is in your court now. Have you received the gift? Are you God's child? Do you know whose you are?

And if you do know God as your Father, I trust that by now you're ready to accept the gift of singleness that He has so graciously given you.

In the next section of the book, I'm going to give you five

attitudes that every single Christian needs in order to thrive. I'll follow that with four obstacles that you're going to have to overcome in order to thrive. You'll then be ready to take the next step in making it happen.

Are you ready to keep going?

PART 2

Five Attitudes
to Embrace

2

I Can't Find No Satisfaction: Learning Contentment

Let's get one thing clear: you can't possibly thrive if you don't like what you have.

The first attitude that every single Christian must embrace in order to thrive is the attitude of contentment.

For the longest time in my life, I felt as if contentment was a word that Christians used as a cop-out, a way to deal with life and accept the inevitable lot they'd been handed. Even though I may be a bit more cynical than the average adult, the odds are that you too have struggled with contentment in your life as a single Christian.

The grass always seems greener on the other side. If you're single, you want to be married. If you're married, you want to be single. If you're dating this guy, you wish you were dating that one. If you're young, you want to grow up. If you're old, you daydream about the good old days when you could do hurdles, even though everyone knows that you never could jump over a hurdle. No matter your lot in life, it seems as if you're always just a dollar short of getting exactly what you want.

Most of us spend our lives never fully satisfied, never completely happy, and never resting in contentment with the life that God has given us right here and right now.

Consider this story:

The rich industrialist from the North was horrified to find the southern fisherman lying lazily beside his boat, smoking a pipe.

"Why aren't you out there fishing?" said the industrialist.

"Because I have caught enough fish for the day," said the fisherman.

"Why don't you catch some more?"

"What would I do with them?"

"You could earn more money," was the industrialist's reply. "With that you could have a motor fixed to your boat and go into deeper waters and catch more fish. Then you would make enough to buy nylon nets. These would bring you more fish and more money. Soon you would have enough money to own two boats . . . maybe even a fleet of boats. Then you would be a rich man like me."

"Then what would I do?" asked the fisherman.

"Then you could *really* enjoy life," said the industrialist.

"What do you think I am doing right now?"[3]

If you read this story about this fisherman and find yourself yearning for his kind of contentment, I'm here to tell you that God wants the same for you. If you long for the peace that comes from having enough, you're in a good place.

You've probably figured out by now that no amount of money will satisfy all of your needs, and I hope you've talked to enough married folks to know that no marriage will ever fulfill your deepest longings.

I spent a big part of my twenties reaching for the infamous carrot on a stick: marriage. I assumed it was God's will for my life, because wasn't marriage God's will for every woman? When I eventually found a guy who asked me to marry him, I naturally said yes; a simple three-letter word that would send my life into a tailspin. By God's grace, the engagement ended two weeks before the wedding, and I was finally able to breathe again.

And I learned a very important lesson in my life—that whether you're single and never married, or single and almost married, *you cannot thrive in your Christian life without contentment.*

NO MARRIAGE will ever fulfill your deepest longings.

It shouldn't have come as a surprise to me, a Bible-believing Christian, that contentment is one of the key attitudes for thriving, especially since the apostle Paul stated it so clearly in 1 Corinthians 7. Listen carefully as you read verse 17: "Only let each person lead the life that the Lord has assigned to him, and to which God has called him."

As if knowing that we would need convincing, Paul repeated his admonition in verse 20: "Each one should *remain* in the condition in which he was called."

And again in verse 24: "So, brothers, in whatever condition each was called, there let him *remain* with God." In other words, Paul was saying that if you're married, be married, and if you're single, be single!

I love the simplicity of God's Word. There is no beating around the bush, trying to figure out some hidden meaning. The text is clear and straightforward. In order to thrive as a single Christian, you've got to stop striving and fighting for what you think must be and simply accept God's will in your life today.

You may have noticed the emphasis I put on the word *remain*. *Remain* is a great word. It means to continue in the same state, not wanting anything else. That's the meaning of contentment. It is your complete satisfaction with God's sufficient provision. It is a settled sense of adequacy in what you have been given. Most of us would agree that God wants every Christian to be content. The tension arises for the single Christian, when a chasm widens between what has been given and what is preferred.

Does the struggle sound familiar? It's an agelong story depicted throughout the Bible. Back in the Old Testament, it was the Israelites who always wanted what they didn't have. When they were in Egypt they were dying to get out, but the moment they were out, they started dreaming about the food they'd left behind in Egypt. They were never satisfied, always wishing for what was just beyond their reach.

As long as they wanted what God hadn't given them,

the Israelites could not thrive. God had to teach them, often through difficult circumstances, that unless they became content, they were doomed to fail. What was true for the Israelites in Old Testament days is true for the follower of Jesus Christ today. Without contentment, you will not thrive as a follower of Jesus Christ. There are no exceptions to the rule.

Do you struggle with contentment in your single life? Do you find it hard to be satisfied with the gift God has given you today? Do you question God's wisdom and His ways in your life?

Unfortunately, many single Christians do struggle with a lack of contentment when it comes to their singleness.

For the longest time in the world, I worried that if I told God I was okay with being single, He'd think it meant that I never wanted to get married. Have you ever had that fear? Have you ever worried whether your acceptance of God's plan for your singleness today was your way of giving up on marriage completely? Yet, your contentment today has nothing to do with what happens in your life tomorrow or how God chooses to unfold His will for your life. Your contentment today is simply an act of faith in a God who is always good.

I WORRIED THAT if I told God I was okay with being single, He'd think it meant that I never wanted to get married.

How silly and narrow-minded we can be when it comes to our Lord. How little we know this God we call our Father. God's will for every single Christian is to live a life that is fully satisfied and content. Without it, you cannot thrive. But when you do learn contentment, you will find yourself bearing much fruit for God's glory and kingdom.

By now you should be ready to learn how to embrace an attitude of contentment. But before we get to that, I'd like to point out four seasons in the life of the single Christian when contentment can be a tremendous challenge. My hope is that in identifying some common triggers for discontentment, you will more easily get on the road to embracing contentment in your life.

SEASONS OF DISCONTENTMENT

1. When Couples Gather

I started making a list of the seasons in my life when I find it harder to be content. My list looked a little bit like a Hallmark store: Christmas, Valentine's Day, family reunions, New Year's Eve, work parties, any party, Sunday church services. The longer my list grew, the more I realized that there was one common thread to the list: each occasion listed included a large gathering of people, mostly couples.

No matter how hard single people try to prepare ahead of time, the mental onslaught of discontentment is loudest when couples gather together to celebrate. Yet holidays and parties are an inevitable part of life and culture. An awareness of the difficulty these seasons create for the single Christian can go a long way toward alleviating the discomfort and discontentment that come along with them.

Some married Christians, in an effort to protect the single Christian from more hurt, have opted not to invite single Christians to their parties. This approach, though seemingly loving, is far from it. One of the recurrent wistful complaints I've heard from single people in the church is the sense that they are routinely left out of church gatherings. The battle for contentment must be worked out in every single Christian with or without inclusion at parties. If you're married and reading this portion of the book, be a sport and keep on looking for ways to include the single Christians in your life, and who knows whether you may gain a babysitter in the process.

2. When Everyone Leaves

Frank Sinatra said it best when he sang, "Saturday night is the loneliest night of the week."[4] If you're single, you probably want to include Friday nights on your list of lonely nights as well. Personally, it's Sunday night that bothers me the most.

Sunday night is the night when families typically gather together before the beginning of a new week. It's the night after a busy, fun-filled weekend. Sunday night is the quietest night of the week for most single Christians, and nothing can fully prepare the single Christian for its echoing loneliness.

It's the same feeling that fills your house after the party is over and everyone leaves. You try turning on the television for company, but the quiet of the now empty space gives your mind ample room to dwell on plans that have never taken shape, dreams that have never become realities, and regrets over past mistakes. Frankly, late at night, any night of the week brings along its set of regrets and unfulfilled longings that create a challenge for most single Christians. It is difficult to be content when people leave, and impossible to thrive in such an environment of discontentment. Identifying this common trigger for discontentment will take you far in your battle for contentment.

3. When People Say Too Much

I've called the third season that will challenge the single Christian's struggle with contentment, "When People Say Too Much," but maybe I should have called it, "When You Listen to Unsolicited Advice from Happily Married Couples and Nosy Third Cousins."

For better or for worse, every Christian single has an uncle with an opinion on why you're still single. You can picture his face right now. He's quick to blame your upbringing or your excessive pickiness for your singleness. He's quick to dish out advice. He's quick to take you down!

How easy it is to get caught up in what people say and forget to focus on what God has said. Sadly, most people speak without seeking God's opinion on matters and end up giving you their own personal opinions instead of the truth of God's Word. I've learned the hard way that the less I hear from others and the more I focus vertically on God's voice, the better off I am and the more content I remain.

Unsolicited advice can surprisingly also come from your Christian single friends. Remember the last time you went out with a group of singles from church? I bet no one had anything to say about your singleness, right? You get my drift. Be careful when people say too much. The old Sunday school song went something like this: "Oh be careful little ears what you hear." There's more truth in that line than you think.

4. *When Other Single People Marry*

The last roadblock to contentment for most single Christians is anytime another single Christian marries. This would be a good time for me to mention my token single guy. Every single woman has one. He's the guy you secretly know would be your perfect husband. You build your dreams around him. You picture your babies' faces that look a little bit like him. He's your perfect guy if only you would meet him.

WHEN OTHER SINGLE people marry, it's easy to feel like God has overlooked you.

I remember how discontented I felt after finding out that my token single guy had gotten engaged, and how happy I felt a few months later when I'd heard through social media that he'd ended his engagement. Oh, and did I mention that my token single guy lives about 3,000 miles away from me and doesn't even know I exist?

It seems silly when I write it, doesn't it? Yet more single Christians than I can count have fallen prey to the news of other singles' impending marriages. When other single people marry, it's easy to feel like God has overlooked you or that you will never get your turn. Focusing on others' good fortune can also bring up feelings of jealousy and envy, both of which are sinful and will only exaggerate the defeat you feel in your life.

Watch out when your single friends get married. It may be a good time for you to guard your heart just a little bit more closely.

Well, we've answered the questions of *when* singles struggle with contentment. I think it's time to go over some common reasons for discontentment that single Christians face.

REASONS FOR DISCONTENTMENT

1. You're Too Focused on Yourself

I spend way too much time overanalyzing and dissecting every aspect of my life. I get too focused on what I want. I'm not that different from my fourth-grade nephew who will often admit, "I don't like what I have," and "I want a different color," or "I want more of this." It's all about me, me, me.

The problem with this approach to life is that when your eyes are on yourself, your vision is restricted and your ability to see everything else is greatly diminished. When self is the focus, problems become magnified, hope is diminished, and discontentment takes over.

Most Christians tend to think far too much about self, or they tend to think far too little about self, never living up to their own expectations of what they think they ought to be. Either extreme is sinful and rooted in pride. A biblical view of self elevates Christ as the standard and puts self in its proper place at the foot of the cross.

In 1 Corinthians 7:23, Paul reminded us of who we truly are in Christ when he said, "You were bought with a price."

Earlier in 1 Corinthians 6:19–20, Paul had already told the Corinthian Christians the same thing, but it seems they needed a reminder.

So how should the single Christian think about self? I believe Jesus said it best in Luke 9:23. Here's what He said: "If anyone would come after me, let him deny himself and take up his cross daily and follow me."

A BIBLICAL VIEW of self elevates Christ as the standard and puts self in its proper place at the foot of the cross.

The answer to your "self problem" is to simply forget about yourself! If you want to thrive as a Christian and grow in contentment, you've got to start by viewing yourself with the right biblical perspective.

2. You're Too Focused on Others

Maybe your struggle isn't about what you want, but what others have. When your eyes are too focused on others, you soon become obsessed with what they have and what you don't. My nephew would say it like this: "Why did she get a bigger piece of pie?" and "How come he always goes first?" You get the picture, and it ain't pretty.

Although you may not be in the fourth grade, you're likely prone to the same temptation. Let me explain. The surest way to be miserable in your life is to turn on the computer, get on Facebook, and spend the next thirty minutes browsing other people's wonderful lives, because everything on Facebook is always so wonderful.

While I have nothing against Facebook, there is no easier way to sink into the pit of discontentment than to spend some time placing all of your attention on your perception of other people's lives.

No matter how great you are, there will always be someone greater. No matter how pretty you are, there will always be someone prettier. And no matter how rich you are, there will always be someone richer.

The quickest ticket to discontentment is the one that takes all of your focus and attention away from the Lord and puts it squarely on other people's lives. It's a lose–lose situation.

3. You're Too Focused on Desire

One of the things that may be adding to your confusion is the problem of your own desires. You want to be married so badly that you can't imagine how God fits into the picture. Why would a good God give you a godly desire and not meet it? You must choose. What will win? Will it be your desire for what you want, or your desire for what God has lovingly given?

When the thing you desire, even if it's good, exceeds your love for God, contentment vanishes and thriving is impossible. Though your desire for marriage is not sin, it becomes sin when you make it essential for your happiness.

Nothing will drive the spirit of discontentment more than focusing so much on your desire and forgetting about

God. Perhaps you've forgotten all about God's goodness and His perfect plan for your life. You've forgotten that God has given you singleness as a gift, and that you were meant to live abundantly no matter the circumstances you've found yourself in.

I think about all the things in my life that I want but don't have—most of which are God-honoring and God-glorifying. I want this book to be used by God to bring Christians closer to Him. Not a day goes by when I don't feel like I want to accomplish more for God. These desires are not sinful in and of themselves, but they become sinful if they take over my heart. In the same way, marriage—though a good thing—can steal your heart, robbing you of joy.

It's easier in such instances to forget all about God.

Fortunately for us, God is not so easily forgotten. He is still in control of every aspect of our life. He is still working out His perfect plan for us. He wants to become the very heart of our desire. He says so in Psalm 37:4: "Delight yourself in the Lord, and he will give you the desires of your heart."

I know this verse can become cliché and overused at Christian singles meetings, but it's God's promise to you and it's true. God's plan for you is to give you the desires of your heart. It is in trusting His Word that you will find contentment.

GOD'S PLAN FOR you is to give you the desires of your heart.

My favorite fable of all time is the one about the dog with a piece of meat in his mouth. He gets to a pond and sees his reflection in the water. The dog becomes so obsessed with the image of a piece of meat in the water that he lets go of the one in his mouth, trying to get the other piece too, but ends up losing both the real piece of meat and the image, finding out the hard way that he's fallen victim to his own desire.

Are you guilty of the same? Are you so focused on your desire that you can't see anything else? Or are you ready to embrace an attitude of contentment? I'd like to end this chapter by giving you four steps that will help you grow in contentment.

FOUR STEPS TO CONTENTMENT

I like to fix things. Give me a problem, and I'll give you a solution. That's not unusual for an ER doctor, and the more I read about Paul's approach to life, the more I am convinced he'd be a great fit in the ER, too. In 1 Corinthians 7:17–24, Paul moves from the problem of discontentment to give us four simple steps for developing an attitude of contentment. Here's how:

1. It's a Matter of Obedience

God doesn't mince words. He gives us each word in His Book for a reason. With that in mind, consider 1 Corinthians 7:17 with me: "Only *let* each person lead the life that the Lord has assigned to him."

Paul repeats this phrase in verse 24 too where he says, "So, brothers, in whatever condition each was called, there *let* him remain with God."

The emphasis on the word *let* in both verses is mine, but the meaning is clear. Paul isn't suggesting contentment as an option. He uses the active verb to strongly point to the necessity of exercising our will in this matter. The verb *let* means "to make" or "to cause to."[5] Contentment is not simply a suggestion; it is a command from God for every single Christian. You must accept the life that God has called you to. If you're married, be married. If you're single, be single. But whatever you do, put your heart and mind into it and actively embrace it by faith.

Paul then compares obedience in contentment to the obedience of circumcision in verse 19, when he says, "For neither circumcision counts for anything nor uncircumcision, but *keeping the commandments* of God."

Again, the emphasis is mine, but the point is clear. God cares about your obedience more than He cares about your outward appearance. When you embrace the attitude of contentment, you are willfully showing your obedience to the Lord. It is an attitude that is based not on your circumstances being what you desire them to be, but on what the Lord has provided for you today.

Your ability to embrace contentment will grow over time. What feels scary and unreachable to you right now will become more natural as you submit to the Lord in obedience, even when it doesn't make sense.

2. It's a Matter of Acceptance

So you've determined to exercise contentment as an act of your will, now let's move to the second step toward embracing an attitude of contentment: accept what you have.

I like to say it another way: *want what you have.* Do you ever catch yourself wanting the one thing you can't have? We're so much like Eve, with closets full of stuff, but always yearning for the one thing we don't have.

YOUR SINGLENESS is not a mistake. It is God's plan for your life today.

Eve had no contentment despite all that God had given her. She went after the one thing she didn't have and fell straight into the pit of sin. The only way out of it was God's saving grace. If you're living your life with a nagging desire for the one thing you don't have, maybe it's time you call it what it is—sin—and confess it right now. Ask the Lord to forgive you and give you the grace to embrace the life He's called you to live.

3. *It's a Matter of Worship*

It's time for a perspective check. This God we call "Father" is the One who called the world into existence. He spoke our universe into being. He oversees every aspect of our lives and our Milky Way. There is not a hair on your head that He has not counted. There is not a secret in your heart that He does not know. He is bigger than your biggest imagination of Him. He is higher than your highest thoughts of Him. My pastor likes to say that God is running the universe with His feet up. How true that is.

He's the God of the Israelites. He's the God of Jacob. And He's the God of you and me.

He's also the God who has called you to your life as you know it. I know this to be true because God repeats different forms of the word *called* seven times in 1 Corinthians 7:17–24. That's a lot of repetition. Listen, your singleness is not a mistake. It is God's plan for your life today.

Will you choose to exalt God for who He is? Will you worship Him no matter what? When you do that, you will find that contentment will come just a little bit more easily and more naturally for you.

4. It's a Matter of Endurance

The last step to embracing an attitude of contentment is to endure with God.

In 1 Corinthians 7:20 and 24, Paul, in reference to the calling God has given each of us, instructs us to remain. Here's what he says: "Each one should remain in the condition in which he was called. . . . In whatever condition each was called, there let him remain with God."

To remain means to stay. To stay, when you feel like leaving, is not always easy. It takes mental toughness and spiritual tenacity. It takes eyes focused upward and a gaze that's unshaken. It takes determination. It takes grit. It takes the Lord standing by your side—which is why I love Paul's whisper to us at the end of verse 24. Did you hear it? He says this: *"remain with God."*

Remain with God. *With God* makes all the difference in the world. *With God* frees you to be who you were meant to be. *With God* is the answer to all of your fear.

God's presence with you is how you can remain when you feel like moving. God's presence near you is how you can rejoice when you feel like crying. God's presence with you is how you can thrive when you feel like shriveling up and dying. God's presence with you is how you can remain content in the calling God has given you even when you feel like being married.

Contentment is satisfaction with God's sufficient provision. He is adequate to meet all of your needs. Won't you willfully trust Him with your singleness and thrive?

Next, we're going to talk about choosing the attitude of self-control. Every single Christian needs it, including you. So what are you waiting for? Turn the page over.

3

Oops, I Did It Again:
Choosing Self-Control

It's no secret that single Christians like to talk about sex. They like to think about sex. They like to whine about sex. They like to idolize sex. In case you haven't picked up on it yet, this is the obligatory sex chapter.

The thing about sex is that it reminds me a little bit of scabies. Not many Christians like to talk about it openly. It's easy to catch, and once you get it, it's harder to get rid of than you think. And it's extremely contagious.

Yet in order to thrive, every single Christian has to understand how to manage his or her own sexual impulses. We're discussing attitudes we need to embrace in order to thrive as single Christians, and the next attitude we're going to cover is the attitude of self-control.

Whether you've had multiple sexual partners or you're still a virgin, chances are that you're carrying your own set of sexual baggage that needs to be measured against God's Word. You can blame the culture or you can blame God for it, but the bags are yours until you figure out what to do with them.

Before you start feeling sorry for yourself, let me remind

you that the church in Corinth understood the added strain of living as a Christian in a sexually inflamed culture. People in Corinth liked sex a lot. They liked to cross-dress, they liked to live together, they fornicated and pornicated—wait, that's not a word, but you get the point. Corinth was not a place you took your mother for vacation. It was a city immersed in sensuality and sexual immorality.

It shouldn't surprise you then that the church in Corinth was affected by the powerful lure of sex. The church had many questions for Paul about proper Christian behavior, including whether or not a guy could sleep with his stepmother! Of course Paul didn't waste any time in explaining exactly how Christians ought to behave toward one another and still honor the Lord Jesus Christ.

Paul's basic premise to the unmarried followers of Christ was this: exercise self-control or get married. I'm not making this stuff up. Here's exactly how Paul said it in 1 Corinthians 7:8–9: "To the unmarried and the widows I say that it is good for them to remain single as I am. *But if they cannot exercise self-control, they should marry.* For it is better to marry than to burn with passion."

Paul's meaning couldn't be any clearer. Incidentally, the problem of self-control isn't restricted to sexual impulses. Your struggle may be with food or self-image or a number of other vices, but Paul's context in this verse is clear. Single Christians will struggle with self-control when it comes to lust. Lust threatens to destroy them if not managed biblically. The biblical solution is this: You got a problem with self-control? Find yourself a wife or husband.

That should be no problem, right? If you're like me, you're

probably a bit miffed at Paul's seemingly simple solution. *Get married? Like I haven't tried that one! I've been engaged twice and just recently found myself on three separate Internet dating sites with absolutely no luck. Easy for you to say, Paul!*

How then must the single Christian, immersed in a sex-inundated culture, face this battle with self-control? For many single Christians, the problem is too big to handle. You have unchecked desires, unmet needs, and unfulfilled longings. Your passions seem too big to manage, but there is no one around for you to hurry up and get married to.

Instead of growing in self-control, you find yourself with little or no control whatsoever. Instead of purity, you know you're full of lust. Instead of thriving, you find yourself ashamed and hiding, afraid of being found out.

So you improvise and tell yourself lies.

LIES SINGLE CHRISTIANS
TELL THEMSELVES ABOUT LUST

1. A Little Bit Won't Harm Me.

Patients will sometimes ask me how much poison will kill them. The answer I give them is obvious: stay away from all poison! The Christian who dabbles in lust is like a peanut-allergic kid who tries just a lick of peanut butter to see what happens. It doesn't matter how you dress it up, he's still ingesting peanuts and could die from anaphylaxis. Lust is not a diet you can control. It is a sin that must be cut off.

2. It's Not That Big of a Deal.

You may be thinking that Paul is just a little too dogmatic for your taste, a little too legalistic. Surely he isn't being literal in his advice to singles in the church. Surely the church in Corinth didn't have the same lame singles group you find yourself stuck in. You tell yourself that it must have been easier to exercise self-control before the advent of television and the Internet. You lie to yourself and convince yourself it's no big deal, until you're caught with your hand in the cookie jar or in an Internet chat room with someone you know.

LUST IS NOT a diet you can control. It is a sin that must be cut off.

What starts as an innocuous habit to relieve stress soon morphs into a self-destructive drug that won't let you go. Pretty soon you hardly even recognize yourself. You're a shell of the person you used to be. Trust me friend, uncontrolled lust is a big deal, every single time.

3. No One Will Ever Find Out.

Ask the five-year-old who was just busted for stealing a cookie, or the pastor whose affair was just unveiled before his entire congregation: secrets have a way of becoming known. You may have heard the slogan, "What happens in Vegas stays in Vegas." Wrong! God's presence reaches even to Vegas. God says it like this in Numbers 32:23: "Be sure your sin will find you out." I don't care what you did last night, God knows exactly where you were and how far things went. Check this verse out in Jeremiah 23:24: "Can a man hide himself in secret places so that I cannot see him? declares the Lord. Do I not fill heaven and earth?" Both of these questions are rhetorical in nature. The answer to the first question is, "No. You cannot hide yourself from God." And the answer to the second questions is, "Yes, God does fill the heaven and the earth." God knows everything. He sees everything. Your secret sin will eventually be made public, and when it does, it will affect everyone around you. I'm not telling you this just to scare you, but because there is a better way to live.

4. Everyone Is Doing It.

This lie is so juvenile that you used it back in the first grade, but it still seems to work, because you're still using it. You figure a little bit of passion is okay because everyone else is doing it too. Furthermore, your unrestrained passion is far less X-rated than that new guy you just met in your small group. Call it what you will, you're still lying to yourself. Even if everyone else is doing it, when it comes to your sin, God is only interested in you.

5. No One Else Struggles with This.

The last lie you will tell yourself is the one that will keep you in the dark the longest. You convince yourself that you're the only Christian you know who struggles with lust. Perhaps out of shame, you choose the safety of silence rather than the freedom of confession, and you persist in your lust. If you believe no other Christian has ever struggled with lust to the extent that you're struggling, I'm pretty sure you haven't read the Bible very carefully.

The Bible is full of people who love sex and struggle with lust to their near destruction. Take Samson as an example, or King David—a man after God's own heart. Their struggle was just as real as yours is, and in every single case, God reached down in love and poured His grace on His children, delivering them from a pit that was too deep for them and a life that was never meant for them.

Look—I'm a forty-year-old virgin, and I know what it feels like to struggle with lust and poor self-control. I also know that God has made a way out for every single Christian, and until you choose self-control, you have no chance of thriving as a Christian.

SO WHAT IS SELF-CONTROL?

Purely defined, *self-control* is "restraint exercised over one's own impulses, emotions, or desires."[6]

SELF-CONTROL IS not your human effort to try to be good.

I like John Piper's take on self-control. He says, "The very concept of self-control implies a battle between a divided self. It implies that our 'self' produces desires we should not satisfy but instead 'control.' We should deny ourselves and take up our cross daily, Jesus says, and follow Him. Daily our self produces desires that should be denied or controlled."[7]

What Piper is saying is that not every desire we have is a God-given one. We have carnal desires left over from our flesh before we came to Christ. The mortification of our carnal desires ought to take place as we grow in our walk with the Lord. As fleshly desires are killed, the Holy Spirit gives us new desires that should take root and grow.

Self-control isn't something you can achieve on your own simply by trying really hard. In Galatians 5:22–23, Paul describes self-control as a fruit of the Spirit. If you know one thing about fruit, it's that the fruit of a tree is decided by the root. You can't manually add fruit to each branch on a tree no matter how hard you try. In like manner, the fruit of the Spirit grows out of a thriving walk with the Lord. The Christian whose heart has been transformed by Christ will bear fruit to show it. As you grow in your walk with the Lord, this fruit should become more and more evident in your life.

That's huge.

In other words, self-control is not your human effort to try to be good. It's not your attempt at holiness that becomes better the harder you try. It's not even your ability to stick to a list of dos and don'ts by sheer grit.

No. Self-control is the fruit born out of your walk with the Lord. Isn't that a relief?

Let me summarize what we've learned so far. When it comes to self-control, the single Christian has just two options:

1. Get married
2. Exercise self-control

We've established that self-control is necessary for the thriving single life. Further, self-control is not something you can manufacture. It is the result of God's Spirit living in the follower of Jesus Christ, producing self-control in the form of increasing fruit.

Now it's time to discuss common areas of struggle with self-control that every single Christian faces.

MASTURBATION

Congratulations. You've found the section of the book on masturbation. It's usually the part of a book on singleness that every single Christian will look for first. If you agree with the author on the topic, you'll finish reading the book. If you don't, it's been real, see you later.

Christians get in a tizzy about masturbation. Is it right? Is it wrong? Can married people do it? And if they can, why can't singles do it? It only seems fair. And what does the Bible say about it anyway?

The statistics on masturbation are staggering. Pretty much everyone's done it at least once, if not once a month. If you're in a dating relationship, you're more likely to masturbate than if you're not dating anyone.[8] Christians hate talking about it. Parents treat it like the plague. Feminists think mentioning it is a rite of passage into the world of cool. Pastors blush when the word is uttered.

The average age most people begin masturbating is 13.45 for men, and 12.75 for women.[9]

I'm pretty sure I was ahead of that curve by at least a couple of years. I'm also pretty sure I've spent the last thirty years fighting off the guilt of repeated failure, and take my word when I tell you that nothing will keep you from thriving like carrying a bag of guilt wherever you go.

If your struggle with self-control boils down to this one

issue, sit up straight and take in the two statements I'm going to make:

You will not die if you masturbate. For the longest time in my life, I thought the verse in Matthew about cutting off your right hand if it causes you to sin was in reference to masturbation. I was wrong. Masturbation is not the unpardonable sin. Sadly, many single Christians have discounted themselves from a life of serving the Lord and impacting their culture because of the sense that they have committed the unpardonable and are beyond redemption or usability by God. Christ died for your sins, every single one of them, including your sin of masturbation. You will not die if you masturbate, but you will find it difficult to thrive until you deal with it.

And then here's the second statement you need to hear: *You will not die if you do* not *masturbate.* You may have heard somewhere that masturbation is natural, and that without it you are stifling some natural physical urge, bringing yourself great harm. That's a lie. Let me be the first doctor to tell you that you will survive if you never masturbate another day in your life. You will not spontaneously combust and self-destruct. You can live happily as a single Christian without ever masturbating again.

YOU WILL NOT die if you masturbate, but you may find it difficult to thrive until you deal with it.

God wants to control every part of your mind, body, and soul. Remember that if you're a follower of Jesus Christ, then you are not your own. You were bought with a price. Your body is a temple of the Holy Spirit. God's plan for your life is not to simply hang on for dear life under the rule of your physical needs. You were made for more. You were made to thrive and live an abundant and free life, with God as your only master. His way is, by far, the better way.

It may be time for you to come to terms with these four facts about masturbation:

1. *It almost always involves lust.* Most people, especially women, cannot masturbate without first developing lustful thoughts. This is usually accomplished by looking at lustful pictures, reading lustful books, or fantasizing about lustful things. The Bible is clear about lust. It is sin, and in time will lead to death (James 1:14–15).

2. *It is an addictive issue of the heart.* Masturbation is not simply a physical act but also a sign of spiritual dysfunction. If you're struggling with uncontrollable masturbation, you may have forgotten the goodness of God to you. You may have developed a spirit of rebellion and a desire to take things in your own hands (no pun intended). If you find yourself habitually masturbating, ask yourself what it is about your view of God that has gone awry and pray for a spirit of repentance instead.

3. *It is all about serving yourself.* Everything about masturbation is self-centered. After all, if you boil it down to the basics, masturbation is having sex with yourself. When you take matters into your own hands and refuse to wait for God's plan to unfold in your life, you stop serving the Lord

and start serving yourself. That's not a very good idea.

4. You will reap what you sow. Stop telling yourself that you will stop masturbating the minute God provides you with a perfect partner. Your habit of frequent masturbation will affect your married sex life. We all reap what we sow. Decide to deal with the heart of the matter now and spare yourself more trouble in the future.

If you're finding satisfaction in your life by gratifying yourself, the odds are that your intimacy with the Lord is suffering greatly too. Your life will not thrive until you put to death this habit and turn to the Lord for healing. Purity is possible, no matter what your past looks like and no matter how many times you've failed before. You were made for more than a lifetime of slavery to lust.

PORNOGRAPHY

The statistics are truly staggering. It's a billion-dollar industry, and it's not just a male problem. Even Oprah thinks it's a problem: "Something's going on in bedrooms across America," she says. "It has been reported that one in three consumers of online porn in our country are now women."[10]

Pornography is everywhere: television, the Internet, ebooks, movies, billboards. We live in a sex-crazed society. It doesn't matter if you're a man or a woman, rich or poor, pornography has woven itself into the very fiber of our culture. Our culture has been pornified, pushing the limits of our sight—both real and imaginary—and most of us have been too busy to notice.

No one is safe anymore, and it's especially difficult to be a single Christian in a pornified culture. It's like swimming upstream in Niagara Falls. It takes miraculous effort. It takes supernatural ability to survive. It takes God on your side and in your heart. It takes friends who have been there and been rescued. It takes time on your knees and a heart that is soft. It takes the willingness to say no and the courage to live differently. It takes simply saying no when it feels so good to say yes.

Despite the immorality in the city of Corinth, Paul thought it possible for the Corinthian Christians to live purely, and by God's help, so can you. It's time to make a choice. Will you walk in the dark or will you turn on the light of God's truth? It's not too late to turn your life around. It's not too late to turn your culture around. You can still thrive in the midst of a pornified society.

I found myself a near casualty of my desires once. It took me by surprise. It came out of nowhere. It wasn't through the Internet or on the TV. It was through an unexpected, even respectable, venue.

I stumbled around a bit, thinking I could handle it. I couldn't. The lure is too strong, the flesh too weak. I tried to minimize it. I tried to justify it. I tried to deny it.

But I knew the truth. Pornography in all of its forms is sin, and it must be cut off.

Once in a while, I get a patient in the ER who won't stop bleeding. It's not rocket science. There's only one way to stop the bleeding: apply direct pressure to the obvious site while you look for the hidden source of the bleed. Surround yourself with a great trauma team. Stick to the protocols.

God's Word is the protocol. Stick to it. Spirit-filled Christians are your trauma team. Befriend them. The obvious sites of bleeding are those things that trigger your fall: a television show, an Internet site, an ebook. Kill those obvious triggers definitively and find a good friend to hold you accountable in it. The less-obvious sites are harder to identify: loneliness, disappointment, fear, rejection. You still eventually need to deal with those triggers or the bleeding will never stop, and your soul will continue to crave what is not holy.

OUR CULTURE has been pornified, pushing the limits of our sight—both real and imaginary—and most of us have been too busy to notice.

It's an all-out war against the culture. It will take every Christian single refusing to laugh when everyone else does and refusing to look where everyone else is staring. It will take every single Christian going back to the place where we are shocked by porn.

In 1 Corinthians 7:5, in talking about sexual temptation, Paul says this: "So that Satan may not tempt you because of your lack of self-control."

Satan has no mercy. He will kick you when you're down. He will laugh when you've blown it. He will stab you in the back. And he intends to win.

But he never will, because Christ has already defeated him on the cross. That's our secret weapon. Paul understood the importance of self-control in a pornified culture. Do you?

FORNICATION

As I mentioned earlier, there is only one plausible solution for the Christian who struggles with self-control: get married. Paul said that because he understood the lure of sex and the danger of lust. Fornication was common in Paul's day, and you can bet it's common now.

Fornication is sex between two unmarried people. Adultery is sex between a married person and someone other than their spouse. Odds are that you know people who are fornicating right now, like for example, any couple you know who is living together outside of marriage. Did you know that 80 percent of unmarried evangelicals ages eighteen to twenty-nine have had sex?[11] That's a pretty high statistic for a Bible-believing group of people. But it may not surprise you as much as it should.

Avoiding fornication is not as easy as it sounds, but not doing so will slowly kill you. The single Christian who plays with the fire of uncontrolled passion is like a frog in boiling water. It dies slowly without even noticing.

The bottom line is that if you're single and you're sexually active, you're fornicating. Kay Arthur likes to say, "Fornicators and adulterers will not inherit the kingdom of God." She's right. She didn't make it up. It's in the Bible, in 1 Corinthians 6:9–10. If you're fornicating, I don't have any good news for you except this: you can still repent and change.

If you're thinking I sound a bit "John the Baptist" to you, you need to consider whether you truly know the Lord as your Savior. God is direct about the truth, and this one is pretty obvious. If you're looking to thrive as a single Christian, there is absolutely no room for sex outside of marriage. Paul's answer to you is simple: if it's that hard to stay pure, marry the guy.

UNCHECKED BOUNDARIES

You tell yourself you'll just cuddle for a minute, but the next thing you know you're touching places you shouldn't touch and feeling things you shouldn't feel. Every single Christian knows the tension of unchecked boundaries in dating.

I added this category to common areas of struggle for the single Christian because many single Christians who date pat themselves on the back for not going all the way and yet do everything short of actual intercourse by the time the evening is over.

If you're reading this and wondering how far you can go and still be pleasing to God, I'm afraid you're asking the wrong question. The Christian life is not about how close to the fire you can walk and not be burned. The Christian life is about seeing how close to the Lord you can walk and thrive.

IF YOU'RE LOOKING to thrive as a single Christian, there is absolutely no room for sex outside of marriage.

Perhaps it's time you stop wondering if petting, or fondling, or kissing, or frenching, or oral is okay. Instead, why don't you use these questions to check your boundaries?

+ Would you do it in front of your parents?
+ Would you do it in front of your small group leader?
+ Would you do it if Jesus were there?

If the answer to any of these questions is no, the odds are that you're going too far.

UNRESTRAINED SENSUALITY

The last area where singles struggle with self-control is in the area of unrestrained sensuality. Unrestrained sensuality is the unrestrained indulgence in sensual pleasures. When it comes to unrestrained indulgences, you may be pushing the boundaries in one of these four areas:

1. What You Wear

Do you aim to attract men's attention in your dress or are you mindful of the effect your outfit has on the opposite sex? A woman recently told me that her husband, in his battle against porn, asked another woman in their small group to dress more modestly. Instead of agreeing with the man's request, the small group kicked the man and his wife out of the group. How tragic that we hold our personal rights and freedom in Christ above the fight for purity of our fellow brothers and sisters in Christ. Is your goal in your dress to land a date by stirring the passion in your ideal man's mind? Or is your goal to be fully pleasing to God? If you're playing this game, friend, beware. You may be closer to the fire than you think.

2. *What You Watch*

While you may avoid pornography and masturbation like the plague, you may be more attached to your sensuality than you think. Take a moment and think about the kinds of shows that you see on TV. Are you careful with what you place before your eyes? In Psalm 101:3 David said, "I will not set before my eyes anything that is worthless." Can you say the same? Although historically, men have been accused of being the more visual creatures, I find that women have become equally enticed by their eyes. So be careful little eyes what you see.

3. *What You Read*

Women, especially, are pushing the sensuality boundaries with the materials they read. With the advent of e-readers, most Christians have access to a number of books that are anything but Christ honoring. Many of those books are given away for free. What book publishers know is that, especially for women, the lure of lust is in the story. When you fill your mind with useless and smutty stories, you will get useless and smutty results. When you fill your mind with Christ-honoring material, you will thrive. You decide.

4. *What You Think About*

It's been said that what you think is who you are. I recently asked a fourteen-year-old patient why he tried to choke himself. Here's what he said: "Well, at first I thought about it for a while, then I just did it."

No truer words have ever been uttered. What you think about will eventually determine how you act. In Romans 12:2 God tells us to not be conformed to this world, but be transformed by the renewal of [our minds]. The transformed mind is the renewed mind, and it is the renewed mind that thrives.

As long as sex remains the highest standard of joy in your heart and mind, you will remain empty and dissatisfied and your life will remain far from thriving. Your soul will never find complete satisfaction no matter the position or the frequency or the depth of intimacy with another person.

You were made for more. Will you start believing it?

SO HOW DOES THE SINGLE CHRISTIAN DEVELOP SELF-CONTROL?

1. Get Down on Your Knees

Before you do anything else, you may need to take some time alone with the Lord and repent. If you've felt a sense of separation from the Lord and a lack of intimacy with Him, it could be because you're harboring sin in your life. In Isaiah 59:2 it says that "your iniquities have made a separation between you and your God, and your sins have hidden his face from you so that he does not hear."

You won't feel close to the Lord until you repent. Repentance involves agreeing with God about your sin, and turning away from your sin. It literally means making a 180 and choosing a different direction for your life. The amazing news is that despite our many failures, God is still willing to grant us His mercy and forgive us by His grace. In 1 John 1:9, He tells us that "If we confess our sins, he is faithful and just to forgive us our sins and to cleanse us from all unrighteousness." That's great news. But the verse that I've found even more convicting is in Proverbs 28:13: "Whoever conceals his transgressions will not prosper, but he who confesses and forsakes them will obtain mercy."

Do you want to thrive? Listen to God's Word. Uncover your sin. Then leave it. If not, you will not prosper.

2. Get Rid of the Garbage

If you're serious about overcoming the sinful habits that control you, you need to get serious about getting rid of the garbage in your life. Romans 13:14 says, "But put on the Lord Jesus Christ, and make no provision for the flesh, to gratify its desires."

When God says to make no provision for the flesh, He means it. Get rid of everything that promotes your sinful habits. For some of you, it will mean getting rid of your television or the Internet. I know a guy who struggled with pornography on his smartphone and was so serious about getting rid of sin that he switched back to a flip phone. That's radical, but that's what "make no provision for the flesh" means.

LISTEN TO GOD'S Word.
Uncover your sin. Then leave it.

Personally, my area of struggle has been ebooks. You cannot set safety guards on the Kindle, and much of the reading material you don't even have to buy. For a while I tried to manage it. I deleted the iBooks application but soon discovered the Kindle app. After repeated failure, I finally got rid of my iPad, deleted the Kindle app from my iPhone, and asked a friend to do random phone checks for me to ensure

Thrive

that I'm following through with my decisions.

The Bible describes Satan as an angel of light, a roaring lion, a liar, and cunning (2 Corinthians 11:3, 14; 1 Peter 5:8; John 8:44). Until you get drastic and serious about getting rid of the garbage in your life, you will not taste victory over your sexual impulses.

3. Guard Your Heart

My patio door is protected by a screen. The screen serves as a barrier, sheltering my home from big animals and mosquitos. The best way to protect a home from unusual animals and insects is to keep the screen door tightly closed.

In the same way, your mind is the gateway to your soul. The best way to protect your soul from dangerous animals is to screen the doors to your mind. Jesus said it like this in Matthew 15:18–19: "But what comes out of the mouth proceeds from the heart, and this defiles a person. For out of the heart come evil thoughts, murder, adultery, sexual immorality, theft, false witness, slander." That's why the Bible tells us to guard our hearts, for out of it proceed the issues of life (Proverbs 4:23).

I saw a movie recently about people who penetrate other people's dreams and modify their thoughts subconsciously. People chuckled on their way out of the theater. They rolled their eyes at the improbability of this ever happening in real life. Yet night after night, you sit and stare at a big square box in your home while the screens of your minds remain wide open to any and every kind of assault that is thrown at you.

You may claim to believe that sex is good only within the context of marriage between a man and a woman, yet you

90

giggle and laugh at situational comedies where sex is casual and immorality cute. You claim to hate murder, but make it a habit of enjoying watching people kill other people. You say you hate pornography, but allow your eyes to slowly numb the contents of your brains while image after shocking image is flashed before your eyes in what is claimed to be a "family friendly" show.

It's no laughing matter. It's time to get serious about self-control. Your mind is the gateway to your soul. Guard it. Protect it. Be careful what you allow to come in it.

4. Get a Godly Friend

Accountability is an interesting phenomenon. It's biblical. Most Christians agree with it. But few people really practice it.

First, you have to find a trustworthy friend. That's not always as easy as it sounds, but we tend to make it harder than it should be.

Second, you have to be totally and completely authentic. Stop talking about your respectable sins. Meet one-on-one with your accountability friend over bacon and eggs, and spill it all—every embarrassing, sinful habit of yours. It may take two rounds of eggs to get through all the ugly details, but it will be worth every bit of effort.

Third, make a specific plan of how you'll be held accountable by your friend. This part has to be tangible and concrete. I've already mentioned that I've asked my accountability partner to do random checks on my phone for the Kindle app. I've also asked her to email me on random days and ask me the difficult questions that I need to be asked.

I've found that accountability is not natural, but it becomes easier with time. And it's absolutely necessary in order for you to thrive God's way. If you can't think of anyone in your life right now who you're comfortable being this authentic with, start praying that God will provide that person. That's what I did, and God did provide. If you're serious about victory, I know God will make a way for you too.

MEET ONE-ON-ONE with your accountability friend over bacon and eggs, and spill it all—every embarrassing, sinful habit of yours.

One of the things I do in the ER is to drain pockets of infection called abscesses. Once the pus is removed from the infected area, there is a big hole in the skin. This hole cannot be left open or else the pus will simply reaccumulate in it. Instead, special gauze must be placed in the empty hole to help the healing process along. So far in this chapter, we've opened up the abscess and gotten rid of the pus of sexual sin. Now it's time to fill up the hole with holiness, lest the infection simply reaccumulate.

It's time to go on to holiness. I'm more than ready. I hope you are too.

4

Holy Rollers and the Church Ladies: Embracing Holiness as a Lifestyle

Every Christian who has ever struggled with sexual sin wants permanent victory over it. You may spend a big portion of your time trying to convince yourself that you can thrive while continuing to enjoy your sinful habits, but you can't.

Aren't you tired of living in guilt and shame? Aren't you tired of another day wasted in sexual failure? Aren't you sick of barely surviving in your Christian walk? Do you ever wonder how long God's patience for you will last in the face of your persistent failure?

It sounds too good to be true, this life of victory. It sounds just a little bit like heaven. But it's as real as the sun. And it's God's will for your life today.

God wants much more for you than you dare imagine. He wants you to be free. He wants you to live the abundant life. He wants you to thrive. I'm pretty sure this abundant life doesn't include the repetitive cycle of failure/repentance/victory that you've gotten so familiar with.

The problem with most approaches to victory over sexual sin is that they are focused on getting rid of the garbage and putting off the sin, but tend to forget about filling the hole in your life that is now gaping.

Think of it this way.

You go to the doctor's office for a checkup, and he tells you you're overweight.

He tells you to stop eating junk food, to stop indulging in cakes and cookies and desserts. Oh, and you need to cut down on the carbs. And while you're at it, forget about fried foods and potatoes.

You agree with him about your weight, and pretty soon the entire contents of your fridge are in the big green trash bin. You're okay for about five hours until you start getting hungry again. You open your fridge but find it empty. You start worrying about starving to death. You have two options: you need to buy healthy food, or else you're going to end up sifting through your garbage in hungry desperation.

GOD WANTS much more for you than you dare imagine.

You were made to eat. Eating is not your problem. Hunger is not your problem. Your problem is that you have forgotten to stock your fridge with healthy foods, foods that are good for you. So instead of joy because of taking a few steps in the right direction, all you can think about is how hungry and how cranky you are and what a terrible headache you're developing. I think you see the point I'm trying to make.

Many single Christians get stuck in the same pattern of living when it comes to exercising self-control. They ditch the computer, they exchange their smartphone for an old flip phone without Internet capabilities, they get rid of cable, they do a whole lot of putting off, then wake up one day and notice that they're still starving half to death.

For many single Christians, perhaps even you, your problem isn't that you have desires, but how you are going about filling your desires.

Here's how John Piper summarizes the struggle for victory over lust in his book *Future Grace*. He says, "We must fight fire with fire. The fire of lust's pleasures must be fought with the fire of God's pleasures. If we try to fight the fire of lust with prohibitions and threats alone—even the terrible warning of Jesus—we will fail. We must fight it with the massive promise of superior happiness. We must swallow up the little flicker of lust's pleasure in the conflagration of holy satisfaction."[12]

I am convinced that what Piper describes here is the key to victory over sexual sin.

You can't just tell yourself you shouldn't sin because people will find out, though they may. You can't just tell yourself that you'll try better next time, because left to your own devices, you won't. You can't just tell yourself to stop wanting, because as long as you're breathing, you will want. It's the object of your wanting that needs to be worked out.

Your desires were given to you by God as a means to draw you closer to Him. Your desires are not meant to defeat you. Your desires are a gift that God has given you to draw you into greater intimacy with Him. The road to greater intimacy with the Lord is called your sanctification process, and it is evidenced by an increasing holiness in your life.

We're about to embark on the third attitude that every single Christian must embrace in order to thrive. We're about to talk about personal holiness.

Did she really just say holiness? Did she really just suggest that one of the five attitudes for thriving as a single Christian is to be holy? Like Mother Teresa or some mousy church lady?

WHO, IN THEIR right mind, wants to be holy? Can't we settle for just normal?

You may be tempted to skip over this chapter and run as fast as you can in the other direction. Sure, you know holiness is a biblical concept, and you know that God is holy. Everyone knows that. But the very concept of holiness sounds so tediously boring. It sounds so archaic. It sounds like something you'd pray for in small group to impress your leader. But to actually live that way? Maybe when you're over forty you'll consider it. But not right now. Right now you're too cool to be a holy roller.

Holiness gets a bad rap. It conjures up images of long robes, quiet cathedrals with stained-glass windows, and twenty-one-day fasts. We're living in the twenty-first century. Who, in their right mind, wants to be holy? Can't we settle for just normal?

Unfortunately, many single Christians have misunderstood and misjudged the idea of holiness. Holiness is actually God's plan for every single Christian, and it's His goal for you if you want to thrive.

UNDERSTANDING BIBLICAL HOLINESS

Before we delve into how to develop holiness, I think it would help you to get a clearer understanding of what holiness is, and the easiest way I can explain it to you is by starting with a short list of what holiness is not.

1. Holiness Is Not Legalism

It's easy to confuse holiness with some outward set of rules and regulations that certain conservative brands of Christianity have embraced in an attempt to control their people or give them a false sense of righteousness. Frankly, that is not holiness. It's legalism and it's sin. The Pharisees looked holy on the outside, yet they didn't recognize the Messiah when He stood smack before their faces. If you think you're holy because you listen to certain kinds of music or avoid certain worldly places, I should remind you that Christ Himself was called a friend of sinners and was often found in places and with people that many of us today would consider questionable. Even the apostle Paul, arguably the most "holy" Christian ever to live, would later say this about himself in 1 Corinthians 9:22: "To the weak I became weak, that I might win the weak. I have become all things to all people, that by all means I might save some."

God cares a lot more about the inside of your heart than what you look like on the outside. Ask yourself these questions: What motives are dictating your "holy" activities? Are you looking for man's approval and praise? Are you hoping God sees you and is impressed enough to finally answer your prayers?

In my own life, I've noticed my tendency to embrace holiness right after a season of failure in the area of lust, hoping to earn some additional favor with God. To put it bluntly, I try to manipulate God into loving me and agreeing to still use me for His glory. Nothing is further from holiness than this kind of performance-based Christianity. God's grace is unearned. It is freely given to us through Christ's death on the cross. God in His grace understands our tendency to rely on holiness as a form of legalism and will not allow us to thrive until every root of self-righteous holiness is eradicated from our lives. I'm so thankful for that.

2. Holiness Is Not Asceticism

There's a holiness that some single Christians have embraced that involves living a lifestyle of asceticism in an effort to eschew the dangers of the culture.

An ascetic lifestyle is characterized by restraint from various sorts of worldly pleasures with the aim of pursuing religious or spiritual goals. Unfortunately, just like legalism, asceticism relies on your own works for salvation and for pleasing the Lord.

You may be so ascetic in your pursuits that you have renounced bodily pleasures, including marriage, in an effort to be more spiritual. This practice is not biblical, and Paul clearly states his position in support of marriage as God-given in 1 Corinthians 7:28. The danger with asceticism is that it can be rooted in pride and lose sight of what Christ has freely done on our behalf.

3. Holiness Is Not Punishment

I have to confess that I'm often afraid of God. I don't mean it in the healthy, churchy "fear of God" sense, but I mean it in the "shaking in my boots," "I hope this never happens to me," "I'm really afraid" sense.

I get scared when I read the story of Ananias and Sapphira in Acts 5 and how God killed them for lying. I get scared when I read the story of Uzzah in 1 Chronicles 13 and how God killed him for touching the ark of the covenant.

God's holiness is serious business, and His ways are very mysterious. It's far easier for us to focus on His love and mercy, and ignore the fact that He is a God who hates sin and demands holiness. We are often tempted to make God what we want Him to be for our own comfort, instead of worshiping Him as He truly is and as He reveals Himself to us in His Word.

I want to tell you how warped my mind can be. Because of my guilt over my repeated failure in the area of masturbation, I've sometimes wondered if God has kept marriage from me as a form of His punishment.

That's unbiblical thinking. God is holy and He hates our sin, no doubt about it. But He longs for us to be holy so that we can have unbroken fellowship with Him. Holiness is not a punishment that He imposes on us because of our guilty past.

You did not forgo marriage because of your failure. God already knew the failure you and I would be when He died for us on the tree. Yet He still opened His arms wide and did it. Do you see how amazing His love is? The more I understand who He is, the more I want to be holy. I love Psalm 103:12 and remind myself of it regularly: "As far as the east is from the west, so far does he remove our transgressions from us."

YOU DID NOT forgo marriage because of your failure.

Holiness is not God's punishment to single Christians for past sins and past mistakes. Holiness is the privilege of every follower of Jesus Christ. Holiness is your means to please the Lord. Paul described it like this in 1 Corinthians 7:32 and 34: "The unmarried man is anxious about the things of the Lord, how to please the Lord. . . . And the unmarried or betrothed woman is anxious about the things of the Lord, how to be holy in body and spirit."

What a joy to embrace holiness not as God's punishment but as His gift to every single Christian to draw closer to Him!

4. Holiness Is Not Just for Pastors

I tend to be lazy, and I confess that holiness sounds just a little bit too hard for me. It sounds like something only professional Christians do—like pastors and seminary graduates.

The problem with my theory is that it's not biblical. God calls every single Christian to a lifestyle of holiness. Holiness is not just for academic Bible types or church nerds. It is God's will for every follower of Jesus Christ. Listen to 1 Thessalonians 4:3–4: "For this is the will of God, your sanctification: that you abstain from sexual immorality; that each one of you know how to control his own body in holiness and honor."

I don't think Paul could have said it more clearly. You can stop trying to figure out what God's will for your life is. I just pointed it out to you from God's Word. God's will isn't about what city you should live in or the house you should buy. God's will isn't about which eHarmony guy you should go to stage four with. God's will for your life, above all else, is for you to be sanctified. The way to do it is through abstaining from sexual immorality and embracing holiness.

5. Holiness Is Not Unattainable

Finally, holiness is not unattainable. Holiness is not unrealistic. No, as a matter of fact, holiness is within your reach.

I have been greatly influenced by the writings of Oswald Chambers. Here's what he says about holiness: "The destined end of man is not happiness, nor health, but holiness . . . Do I believe I need to be holy? Do I believe God can come into me and make me holy? The preaching of the gospel awakens an intense resentment because it must reveal that I am unholy; but it also awakens an intense craving. God has one destined end for mankind—holiness."[13]

The bottom line is that holiness is very attainable. It is more than possible. It is your right and your privilege in Christ. Holiness is God's will for every single follower of Jesus Christ, and it is the only way you will thrive as a Christian.

SO WHAT EXACTLY IS HOLINESS?

A great example of holiness is found in the Old Testament, and specifically from the life of Moses. In Exodus 34:29–35 we're given an astounding account of Moses' day-to-day life. Grant it, Moses was a pretty special guy. He led the people of Israel out of Egypt after spending forty years in the wilderness. He was clearly God's chosen man.

While the Israelites were in the wilderness, Moses would regularly separate himself from the people to spend time with God. He would go up to the mountain and speak to God face-to-face, as a man speaks to his friend. Those aren't my words. I borrowed them from Exodus 33:11.

One time, after Moses came down from spending prolonged time in God's presence on the mountain, his face shone so brightly that the people around him were afraid and couldn't even look at him. They had to cover his face with a veil. The interesting thing is that Moses couldn't tell that his face shone that brightly. It just did because he had spent so much time with the Lord, and God's holiness reflected on Moses' face.

From that day on, whenever Moses would go in before the Lord, he would remove the veil, then put it back on when he came out to talk to the people.

Now, I bet you're thinking, *This is a great story, but I'm no Moses.* You're just a single Christian who simply wants to thrive. I get it. I could never be like Moses either. But here's the part of the story I do want you to hear.

While all the people turned their faces away from Moses, one guy did not. In Exodus 33:11, we're told about a young man by the name of Joshua. Here's what the verse says: "When Moses turned again into the camp, his assistant Joshua the son of Nun, a young man, would not depart from the tent."

I get chills every time I read this verse. See, Moses may be too intimidating for most of us to emulate. But consider Joshua. He was still a young man in Exodus 33. I bet he didn't know he was the guy who would take over the leadership of Israel after Moses died. I bet he didn't know he'd march around Jericho and defeat it with the blow of a trumpet. I bet he didn't know that the waters of the Jordan would part for him later on, in the book that would carry his name.

All Joshua knew was that there was a God who spoke to His people, and Joshua wanted a piece of Him. He would take anything he could get as long as he got to know that God just a little bit more—even if it meant staying after Moses left. Even if it meant hovering in the corner of a tent somewhere. Even if it meant simply waiting until God showed up for him.

Now that's what I call running after personal holiness. Are you willing to do what Joshua did? Are you as hungry for the Lord's presence in your life? What are you willing to do in order to see the Lord in your life?

Here's what God promises: when you seek Him like that, He will make Himself known to you. That is a guarantee. So will you do it?

HOW TO GAIN AN ATTITUDE OF HOLINESS

We've established that holiness is necessary for thriving, and we've given a substantive definition of holiness by discussing what holiness is not and discussing the example of Joshua. I think it's time you find out how to grow in the attitude of holiness. I've boiled it down to these five steps:

1. Recognize Who You Are

I get pretty busy in life and tend to forget who I am. So about once a day, I stop and look in the mirror to remind myself of who I am. I check my face, my hair, and my teeth. I may even check my outfit. It only takes a second, but it's necessary and helpful.

The same is true spiritually. You can get so caught up living your life that you forget who you are.

WHAT ARE YOU willing to do in order to see the Lord in your life?

When it comes to your personal holiness in Christ, it's also easy to forget. It's easy to forget that Christ atoned for all of your sin—past, present, and future. It's easy to forget that the shedding of Christ's blood on the cross put you back into perfect union with the Father. It's easy to forget that sanctification is the work of the Spirit living in every follower of Jesus Christ, including yourself.

If you're a Christian, your personal holiness is the result of your sanctification process. It is the result of your adoration of Christ for what He has done for you. If you're a follower of Jesus Christ, you can be holy because of who you are in Christ. If you're a single Christian, you get an even better deal: you get to spend all of the time married people spend on each other to simply focus on the Lord! What a privilege that is.

2. Make Room for Holiness

I have a really small closet. The only way I can fit new clothes in my small closet is to get rid of my old clothes. I discussed this principle in the last chapter, but I'll review it for you again. For you to become holy, you must first get rid of the sin in your life.

In 2 Corinthians 7:1 it says this: "Since we have these promises, beloved, let us cleanse ourselves from every defilement of body and spirit, bringing holiness to completion in the fear of God."

In this passage, Paul had just finished reminding the Corinthian believers that their bodies were a temple of the Holy Spirit. He finishes his thoughts by instructing the Corinthian Christians to make a clean break with anything and everything that distracts or defiles them. This break is not merely an outward one, but primarily an inside one.

There have been times in my life when I've heard sermons on repentance and read books about it. I've agreed with the principles, but when it came to follow-through, I succeeded only for a while. My problem was that I didn't hate my sin enough. Though I said I wanted repentance, I didn't really mean it as evidenced by my quick return to sin, or my incomplete destruction of the thing that caused me to sin. I had a hard time letting go of the sinful thing because I still loved it more than I loved God. I found ways to justify its continued presence in my life. I convinced myself that I could grow in holiness even though I harbored a small closet of sin in my life.

I was wrong.

I had to learn two things: First, that repentance is a gift

that God gives. I began praying sincerely for repentance, and God answered my prayers. Second, I learned that God's Word always trumps my feelings. I don't have to feel like obeying. I simply have to do it. Feelings are terrible leaders, but they make great followers.

I HAD A HARD time letting go of the sinful thing because I still loved it more than I loved God.

True repentance admits that God is right even when you don't quite understand it. You choose to trust God's Word by faith and obey it even when you don't add up the why. That's how you make room for holiness, and that's how you take another step toward the life that thrives.

One of my favorite C. S. Lewis quotes is this: "It would seem that Our Lord finds our desires not too strong, but too weak. We are half-hearted creatures, fooling about with drink and sex and ambition when infinite joy is offered us, like an ignorant child who wants to go on making mud pies in a slum because he cannot imagine what is meant by the offer of a holiday at the sea. We are far too easily pleased."[14]

As single Christians, we resist making room for holiness, thinking that if we did fully embrace holiness we would somehow be giving up on our full sexual potential. We spend far too much time worried about whether God has a solution for our frustrations. Or we try to postpone holiness, hoping for some temporary earthly pleasure, however weak it may seem. Sometimes we try to juggle holiness along with our own version of Christian sensuality. It just doesn't work that way.

God hates sin. Holiness cannot coexist with sin. The good news is that God has much more for His children than any earthly pleasure promises to give. The caveat is that you must take a step of faith in obedience to God's Word in order to fully see the truth of it. I know, because I did. And I hope you will too.

3. Concentrate on Holiness

Have you ever wanted something so bad that you just couldn't stop thinking about it? Like when you were in high school and wanted to go to Six Flags so bad you couldn't think about anything else? You would wake up thinking about it. You would go to sleep with it on your mind. You put all of your concentration on this one thing.

The third step to embracing holiness is to fully concentrate on it with everything you've got. Let's go back to 1 Corinthians 7:32. Here's what it says: "I want you to live as free of complications as possible. When you're unmarried, you're free to concentrate on simply pleasing the Master" (THE MESSAGE).

Free to concentrate on pleasing the Lord. Free to focus on holiness. Free to consider thought, word, action, and motive in holiness. Free to think about what areas of sin still need to be forsaken and what aspects of holiness still must be embraced.

There's a little chorus we used to sing in church that went like this: "Holiness, holiness is what I long for. Holiness is what I need. Holiness, holiness is what You want for me."[15]

Do you long for holiness? Are you fully concentrated on the Lord, like Joshua was, and panting for His presence in your life? Did you know that there are 1,440 minutes in a day, and 10,080 minutes in a week? How many of them are you spending on concentrating on holiness? Sadly, many of us talk about concentrating on God but spend very little time actually doing it.

Maybe it's time to change.

4. Strive for Holiness

The last thing you need to know about gaining an attitude of holiness is that God never promised it would be easy. In Matthew 7:14, Christ describes the Christian road as narrow and difficult. Yet many Christians find themselves slowly meandering off the road, scratching their head, wondering why no one told them life would be so hard.

Let me be clear: the Christian life is not easy. Following Jesus Christ entails picking up your cross daily and following a Savior who hung on that cross. He is our example in every way, including in our suffering.

My favorite verse on holiness is in Hebrews 12:14. The writer says this: "Strive for peace with everyone, and for the holiness without which no one will see the Lord."

This verse is so rich. Did you catch what it says? You may want to read it again. Without holiness you cannot even see the Lord. If you've been struggling to see God in your life, perhaps it's because you are not walking in holiness.

SADLY, MANY OF us talk about concentrating on God but spend very little time actually doing it.

If you look back on the verse in Hebrews 12, I'd like to turn your attention to the word *strive*. I looked it up on Google and here's what I found.

1. To exert oneself vigorously
2. To make strenuous efforts toward any goal
3. To contend in opposition, battle, or any conflict
4. To struggle vigorously as in opposition or resistance[16]

If you're reading this book there's a good chance that you long for holiness in your life and that you long to thrive in your walk with the Lord.

The good news is that that is exactly what God wants for your life too.

The bad news is that it will not be easy.

Are you willing to strive toward holiness? Are you willing to endure tribulation and suffering for the sake of holiness? Are you willing to give up your personal rights and comforts in order to see more of Jesus in your life?

Here's some more good news: you are not in it alone. Christ in you is the One who alone will bring your holiness to completion in the fear of God. His Spirit in you makes it possible.

He is your strength. He is your presence. He is your aim. You are not in this battle on your own. The question is: Are you willing to trust Him with your holiness? Are you willing to trust Him with your life?

5

Free as a Bird:
Understanding True Freedom

On July 19, 1987, my family moved from Beirut, Lebanon, to Green Bay, Wisconsin. It wasn't because we were avid Packers fans. It wasn't because we preferred the northerly winters. And it certainly wasn't because of the Wisconsin cuisine of bratwurst and cheese curds.

No . . . thirty years ago, my father moved our family halfway across the world because we wanted to be free.

We longed to live free of political oppression and economic upheaval. We yearned to live free of fear for safety. We dreamed of a life where individual liberties were not only a topic of conversation at the dinner table, but realities that were embraced and believed.

I was fifteen years old, and I have never looked back.

For those of you who have grown up in the United States of America, the concept of freedom is so mundane, and the idea of independence so intricately woven into the fiber of your souls that to live without it seems out of the question and foreign. Yet for centuries, men and women have given up their lives for the sake of freedom. Battles have been fought for freedom. Men and women have died while crossing the borders of their own oppressed lands to make it into the land of the free.

Freedom.

ONE OF THE greatest gifts of the single Christian life is the gift of freedom.

Songs are written about it. Adolescent dreams are built on it, but most importantly, Christianity hinges on it.

In Galatians 5:1, Paul sums it up this way: "For freedom Christ has set us free; stand firm therefore, and do not submit again to a yoke of slavery."

In Christ, every prison door has been opened. In Christ, every captive is set free. In Christ, every threat of slavery is destroyed. In Christ, you are free to live and free to thrive.

It doesn't matter if you feel free. It doesn't matter if you act like you're free. The reality is that Christ's death on the cross has purchased your freedom forever. Imagine for a minute that after moving from Lebanon, my family had decided to stay in the basement, stockpiling bread and water, the lights kept dim to avert the enemy from knowing our location. You would think we were silly or uninformed. Imagine that after moving from Lebanon, my family chose not to send us to school for fear of the bombs. You'd wonder about our understanding of the Western world, and maybe even our sanity.

Or you'd simply just remind us: You are free! You don't

have to be afraid anymore! You don't have to live in the darkness. You can go ahead and live like you're free!

One of the greatest gifts of the single Christian life is the gift of freedom. Yet some of you are still living out the imaginary scenario I just painted. Instead of embracing the freedom you've been given, you persist in locking yourself up in the basement of your life, counting off days until your sentence is over. Instead of a life of thriving, you are slowly shriveling up—ignoring the freedom that God has so graciously given you in this season of your life.

Paul understood what a gift this freedom was. In 1 Corinthians 7:32–34 he summed up his thoughts on freedom by telling the unmarried Christians this: "I want you to be free from anxieties. The unmarried man is anxious about the things of the Lord, how to please the Lord. But the married man is anxious about worldly things, how to please his wife, and his interests are divided."

It's time we cover the fourth attitude that every single Christian needs in order to thrive. It's time to talk about true freedom. If you're a single Christian, you probably fall on one extreme of the freedom spectrum or the other. You either abhor the freedom that comes with singleness and yearn for the confinement of marriage, or if you're like me, you may have made too much of this freedom.

You love your freedom so much, you dare anyone to tell you what to do. You love your freedom so much, you dare someone to form a deeper relationship with you. You don't mind dating casually but cannot stand the idea of a long-term commitment because of the threat that a man may pose on your freedom.

I know all about that. I was born with a genetic predisposition toward independence. I went to college at sixteen and have lived alone for the last twenty years. I love my freedom—almost to a fault. People typically want to know how I survived breaking off not one, but two engagements. The truth is that I felt relief both times because I knew that I was finally free from entanglements and commitments.

I say this to my shame. Yes, Christ purchased my freedom. Yes, Jesus came to set me free. But Christ didn't die on the cross so that I could do whatever I feel like doing whenever I feel like doing it. My freedom was bought with a price, and it demands my all in return. Christ did not die so that I could live independently for my own self-will and self-glory. He did it so that I could be free to live and to thrive for His glory.

So . . . if Christ did not set me free for my own personal agenda, what exactly does my newfound freedom in Christ allow me to do?

That's a great question. I'm glad you asked it. Before I tell you what you've been set free to do, let's spend the next section looking at what Paul tells us we've been freed from.

FREE FROM WHAT?

1. Freedom from Anxiety

I'm not a complicated person. I take things at face value. When Paul says, "I want you to be free from anxieties," I think he means that the unmarried Christian is to be free from anxieties.

You probably have a pretty good idea what anxiety means, but I looked it up in the dictionary for you anyway.

Anxiety is "distress or uneasiness of mind caused by fear of danger or misfortune."[17] I guess you can call it a state of apprehension. It is a general sense of worry and foreboding.

You may know the feeling well. I know I do. It's what you feel when you get that unexpected tax bill. It's what you feel when you get the phone call in the middle of the night. It's what you feel when you open up your test results and read the news you were dreading. You suddenly feel like throwing up. You feel like you've been punched in the gut. There's a squeezing sensation around your head.

You become laden with anxiety.

There may be a number of things that create anxiety in your life, but nothing magnifies your anxiety as much as other people do. It's why holidays around family gatherings become so stressful. It's why personal retreats in remote areas are so relaxing. Being around other people will inevitably increase the anxiety in your life. You can no longer do what you want to do when you want to do it. You must now consider other people's needs and desires. It's not easy being human around other humans.

THE BIBLE TELLS us not to worry about tomorrow, yet tomorrow has stolen many Christians' joy today.

Now imagine living in extremely close proximity with just one other person for the rest of your life—for better or for worse, in sickness and in health, come what may, until

Christ returns. God calls that arrangement *marriage* and it brings along with it a certain level of anxiety that only married people truly understand, even when they're madly in love with each other.

Let's go back to 1 Corinthians 7. When Paul talks about singleness and marriage, he doesn't tell people to avoid marriage because of the anxiety it adds to life. Quite the opposite: Paul advocates marriage as God-given and good. But here's what Paul does say: being single ought to free you of the additional anxiety that married people have. In other words, if you're a single Christian, you're supposed to have less anxiety, not more of it!

So why do single Christians still live in such a daily state of anxiety?

I believe anxiety is a direct result of your divided interests. It's what happens when you turn away from the Lord and focus on your circumstances. When problems become big, God becomes small, and anxiety increases. The Bible tells us not to worry about tomorrow, yet tomorrow has stolen many Christians' joy today. When you turn your eyes toward your circumstances, the things of the world become your focus, and every one of your problems becomes magnified. You start asking yourself questions like, *Will God ever provide the right man for me? Has God forgotten about my biological clock? How will I have enough for my retirement on just one income? Should I buy a house or keep on renting?*

Whatever it is that is causing your anxiety is stealing your joy and freedom in Christ, and with it, your ability to thrive. It's time you take your eyes off of your circumstances and worldly cares, and fix them firmly on Jesus Christ.

The advantage that the single Christian has is the ability to maintain an undivided interest on the Lord Jesus Christ. The freedom from anxiety that you have as a single person is a direct result of your focusing on the Lord. Rest your eyes fully on the Lord, and peace will ensue. Listen to what Paul said in Philippians 4:6–7: "Do not be anxious about anything, but in everything by prayer and supplication with thanksgiving let your requests be made known to God. And the peace of God, which surpasses all understanding, will guard your hearts and minds in Christ Jesus."

Prayer is your secret for anxiety-free living. God's gift to you as a single Christian is additional time to pray and the freedom to give your undivided attention to Him. Are you focusing your interests on the Lord and experiencing freedom from anxiety? If not, it may be time to start.

2. Freedom from Pleasing Man

Most of us are people pleasers by nature. We long for the approval of others. We strive to make others happy. We live under the dominion of what others think and say about us. It can be even worse if you're single. You look for the opposite sex to define you and yearn for others to affirm you.

But you were made for so much more.

In 1 Corinthians 7:32, Paul holds you by the chin, looks you in the eye, and tells you as directly as he can: make pleasing the Lord your main focus in life. Make it your life goal. It is when you focus everything in you on pleasing the Lord that you will know true freedom. Be free from the weight of pleasing man. The blessing of the single life is that you are free of the need to check with a spouse about which color to paint the walls in the dining room. You don't need your in-laws' opinion on the destination of your next vacation. You, single Christian, are free to live the life God has prepared for you.

If you read the part about arguing over which color to paint your walls and getting your in-laws' input, and immediately think, *Well those would be a nice problems to have, if you ask me,* you're missing the point. You are wasting the freedom that God has given you. The freedom of the single Christian life is a freedom from the constant anxiety of what your significant other wants and thinks. As a single Christian, your main question each day ought to be, *Lord, what do You want me to do today?*

When you ask the Lord this question, you may be surprised how He answers you. I have found two specific areas that God uses single Christians to help build His kingdom.

Financial Freedom

Did you know that if you're single, over seventeen, and working, you can spend your money on whatever you choose to? Some of you know that all too well. You have splurged on your hobbies and spent impulsively, building up credit and using your freedom excessively for your own desires.

But when you shift your interests onto the Lord, your whole life will change. I wonder what it would look like if you started asking the Lord how you ought to spend the resources He has entrusted you with. You will no longer care about building your own little kingdom or buying the latest tech trend. Instead, you will become hungry for God's kingdom to grow.

God may even call you to do something crazy with your finances—like sell your house, store up your savings, and become a missionary. You're probably not that radical, but still . . . God could use you to support a missionary, or build a school in Africa, or even help a child in need. It may be time to let go of your American dream and allow the Spirit of God to move you to do something that will free you from this world and the distractions in it, in order to live the full life that God has for you. Now that's what I call freedom.

Freedom in Your Time

Consider the way you spend your free time. Aren't you tired of eating at yet *another* new restaurant in town with all the single people from church? Aren't you sick of spending your income on yet *another* Hollywood movie and a box of calorie-filled popcorn, numbing your brain with endless entertainment that will reinforce the idea that you'll never be enough? I'm not suggesting that you don't need to relax. But what I am suggesting is that when you stop long enough and ask the Lord how you should be spending your time, the answer may surprise you. True freedom is born out of obedience to God and not self-indulgence. True freedom is yours when you give all of your time to the Lord and see Him bear lasting fruit in your life that abides for eternity. Anything short of this kind of freedom will find you spending your days in a never-ending, futile chase of some hidden rainbow and coming up empty and dissatisfied.

Thrive

WHEN YOU STOP long enough and ask the Lord how you should be spending your time, the answer may surprise you.

In every single decision in your life and in every single situation, you will have to choose: Will you please God or will you please yourself? Your answer will reflect how free you really are.

3. Freedom from Distractions

A look at the life of many single Christians shows not a life of undivided interests, but one of overwhelming distractions: Where should I go on vacation? What should I eat today? Which hobby should I pick up? How many Internet dating sites should I join?

While single Christians may think that widening their interests will make them more marketable in the hunt for a spouse, nothing could be further from the truth. Distractions are one of Satan's greatest ploys to keep the Christian from a life of serving the Lord faithfully. Yet never before have we had as many distractions at our disposal as we do today. We have more television channels than most of us can list. The variety of video game consoles robbing men of years of their lives is paralyzing. We have books to read at the tap of a finger and home libraries stuffed with more unread volumes than ever before. We have social networking, real networking, Internet-dating networking, and church networking. If you've thought about it, odds are there is a blog about it. If you're interested in it, there's most likely an interest group on it.

Is it any wonder that so many single Christians have no idea what to do with their freedom? Consider, on the other hand, the men and women who lived just a generation before we did. Take for example David Brainerd, the great missionary to the American Indians who gave up his life to serve the Lord; or Amy Carmichael, a single Christian woman who moved to India and risked her life to spread the gospel to orphans. Only eternity will reveal how many hearts have been ignited for service by the testimony of the men and women who refused the distractions of their age and lived with their attention fully focused on God's kingdom. These were men and women who understood the freedom of a life without distractions and went after the Lord with all of their mind and heart.

May God raise up a new generation of Christ followers who understand that the single Christian life is a gift that allows greater freedom to serve the Lord. This is freedom without the distraction of family and worldly cares, for the elevation of Christ's great name and the building up of His kingdom!

FREE TO WHAT?

During my thirties, I was living the American dream. I had a condo in downtown Chicago, right off of Michigan Avenue with a great view of the lake. I had a great job running the ER of one of the best children's hospitals in the world. I had a great car, good health, and enough money to do anything I wanted to do. I could date anyone, do anything, go anywhere that I wanted to go.

Yet most Friday nights, I found myself sitting on the sofa in my living room, remote control in hand, trying to decide which made-for-TV movie I wanted to watch.

I like to call that kind of freedom, *wasted freedom.*

If you find yourself free to do anything, but unsure of exactly what to do, you too may have become an expert at wasting the freedom God has given you. It's time to wake up and figure out what you've been freed for!

1. Free to Delight

The first freedom that the single Christian is meant to enjoy is the freedom to love God fully. John Piper is one of the greatest theologians of our generation. He has built his life and ministry on one principle that summarizes what it means to delight in God. Here it is: "God is most glorified in us when we are most satisfied in Him."[18]

You may be reading this chapter so far and be thinking to yourself, *Okay, okay, I get it. I'm supposed to do something for God. All right—I'm on it.* I'm here to tell you that nothing will sooner rob your freedom in Christ than doing work for Christ without delighting in Christ. If you want lasting freedom, you must move from mere duty to utter delight in your walk with the Lord, or you will never thrive as a follower of Jesus Christ.

IS IT ANY WONDER that so many single Christians have no idea what to do with their freedom?

Yes, God wants you to obey and serve Him, but nothing breaks His heart more than seeing you do it merely out of duty. Service for God and obedience to Him must stem out of an overflow of your relationship with Him. When you are fully satisfied in Christ, the result is that you want to serve Him.

Consider the act of reading your Bible. You may think that if you read your Bible daily, God will be pleased with you and will answer your prayers, and may even provide a spouse for you. So you sit down dutifully and cross off your Bible reading for the day, then wonder why you hardly know this great God or enjoy His presence. Pretty soon you begin wondering why your Christian walk feels like a prison that binds you rather than a field that frees you. What you're missing is relationship. What you're missing is simple delight in a personal Savior. The point of reading your Bible each day is to bring you into closer relationship with the One who has purchased your freedom. It is through His Word that you know Him more intimately and understand His will for your life. The freedom that comes with the single Christian life is the freedom to spend unhurried time with the Lord, without the distraction that married people feel. It is a freedom to delight in and to worship the King of kings for all He's done for you.

Life in Christ is most enjoyed when it is a life of delight. King David understood that in many of his Psalms, as he repeatedly lifted up his voice in praise and adoration of the One who gave him life.

Ask most married Christians what they miss most about their single life, and they will tell you that it's the focused, unhurried time they had to spend with the Lord. Though they may still spend time with God, it is often interrupted and heavily fought for.

If you're a single Christian, learn to delight in God. Spend time with Him, seek His face, and ask Him to show Himself to you in fresh ways. You have been given the freedom to know God, a freedom so rich that Paul himself chose not to marry in order to enjoy time of uninterrupted delight in God. What a privilege and blessing we've been given!

2. Free to Love

Our culture has done an amazing job of elevating love more than any other feeling in the world. It's easy to blame Disney for most of our warped ideas about love and "happily ever afters." But deep down, we all yearn to know a love so unconditional and everlasting that nothing will ever break it.

What we have forgotten is that we don't have to marry to know that kind of love. Ask any married person and they'll tell you the truth: marriage doesn't resolve your love problem. Only Jesus Christ does. Only He can meet all of your needs. Only He loves you unconditionally. He's the only One who will never disappoint you and will never waver in His faithfulness to you. He gave Himself for you because of love. You are Christ's big love. And the moment you accepted Him, His love came to live in you. Once you understand Christ's unconditional love, you're ready to love others in much the same way.

I once had a plant that I kept watering over and over again, but it still died. I couldn't figure out why, until a friend suggested I check the pot. There were no holes in the bottom of the pot, which meant that the water I was pouring over the plant had nowhere to go. My plant died because it was overwatered. I called it death by overflow.

Unfortunately, many Christians suffer the same demise. Christ's love is meant to overflow through you and on to others. For the single Christian, that means that you don't need to be married in order to love unconditionally. You were meant to love others right here and right now.

People in our world are hungry for that kind of unconditional love. We are living in days where love is rare and fleeting. People are used to being hurt. They expect it. Yet God's plan for His children is to touch the world with Christ's love and bring the redemptive truth of the gospel to them. People are waiting for the kind of love that endures. They are waiting for a love that stays and is longsuffering and kind. You can convince yourself that you love others, but until you open the door of your heart and let Christ's love overflow toward them, you may be deceiving yourself.

THE FREEDOM that comes with the single Christian life is the freedom to spend unhurried time with the Lord.

I feel like you deserve fair warning: when you love other people freely with Christ's love, you open yourself up to being hurt, maligned, and possibly even rejected. It shouldn't come as a surprise to us though, since our Savior suffered the same response when He demonstrated His perfect love for us. Here's how Peter describes it in 1 Peter 2:21–23: "For to this you have been called, because Christ also suffered for you, leaving you an example, so that you might follow in his steps. He committed no sin, neither was deceit found in his mouth. When he was reviled, he did not revile in return; when he suffered, he did not threaten, but continued entrusting himself to him who judges justly."

That's the kind of love the world needs to see. You, single Christian, are strategically positioned to give it. You, single Christian, have been blessed with a life of great freedom intended for God's glory and His kingdom.

You can adopt babies and foster them. You can travel to underserved areas, giving up six-figure incomes to build churches and schools, and bring healing. You can invite the annoying guy in the next cubicle over for dinner. You can patiently endure the unrealistic requests of a needy family member. Or you can dream up even more extravagant things to do for the sake of Christ.

You are free to love like you never thought possible.

So what are you doing to reflect Christ's love to a dying world? Will you pray right now for God to use you as an instrument to show Christ's love to others?

It is this kind of love that unleashes the life that thrives.

6

Single-Minded Focus: Pursuing Undivided Devotion

I t's time to get your GPS out and recalibrate.

So far in the book, we've talked about what it means to thrive. We laid the foundation for our biblical text from 1 Corinthians 7, and we discussed the gift of singleness with its share of blessings. We then moved on to the *how* of thriving, and spent the last few chapters addressing four attitudes every single Christian needs in order to thrive.

We're now coming up to the fifth and final attitude you need to thrive as a single Christian. This attitude may be the most important of them all. It will certainly demand your unwavering focus. It is the attitude of undivided devotion.

No one understood the importance of single-minded focus like Paul did when he wrote 1 Corinthians 7:35: "I say this for your own benefit, not to lay any restraint upon you, but to promote good order *and to secure your undivided devotion to the Lord.*"

I'd like to remind you of Paul's story. He was a man who was hell-bent on killing every follower of Jesus Christ when the Lord appeared to him and saved him. Paul's meeting with

Christ on the road to Damascus not only radically changed the course of his life, but he never got over the impact of that meeting.

Paul's conversion resulted in his world turning upside down. Everything about his life changed. He hightailed the caravan, headed to Damascus, and embraced a lifetime of devotion to the Lord. Paul wrote about how other Christ-followers responded to Paul's conversion in Galatians 1:23–24. Here's what he said: "They only were hearing it said, 'He who used to persecute us is now preaching the faith he once tried to destroy.' And they glorified God because of me."

If anyone understood the meaning of undivided devotion, it was the apostle Paul. Have you ever wondered why some people seem more devoted to God than others?

Luke 7:36–50 may help you answer that question. Jesus was at a party at the house of a Pharisee named Simon when a sinful woman of the city—otherwise known as a prostitute—suddenly showed up and broke an alabaster flask of ointment on Jesus' feet in worship and adoration of Him. Simon was appalled. How could Christ allow such extravagant emotion, and from a whore nonetheless? Jesus looked Simon straight in the eye and told him a parable. In the parable, Jesus described two people who were forgiven a debt: one guy was forgiven five hundred denarii, while the other was forgiven fifty. Jesus asked Simon which man would he suppose was more thankful. The answer was obvious even for Simon: the guy with the bigger debt was more thankful. Jesus then made His final point and concluded with this: "Therefore I tell you, her sins, which are many, are forgiven—for she loved much. But he who is forgiven little, loves little" (Luke 7:47).

Here was Paul, a man known to murder Christians, going along his merry way when God stopped him in his tracks, forgave him every one of his sins, and gave him a completely new life. Oh, Paul never got over the Lord Jesus Christ. He was a man who understood what it meant to be forgiven much, and his devotion to the Lord was total and complete.

If you're a single Christian, you're probably tracking with my thoughts on undivided devotion, but may be wondering what the connection is between Paul's depth of forgiveness and your singleness.

Good question. The only answer I have for you is this: single-minded focus.

Paul's focus was single-minded because he never forgot what Jesus Christ had done for him. The result was his undivided devotion to the Savior. In the same way, the single Christian's interests ought to also be undivided, with a focus so narrow on Jesus Christ that the result is the same undivided devotion that Paul had.

Sadly, my life tends to be a little more like a Chinese restaurant menu. I get easily lost in the options. Despite the pages and pages of menu, I still never know what to order and always end up ordering something that doesn't look quite as good as I had thought it would, based on the picture I had in my mind.

Do you ever feel that way too?

I find myself easily distracted and out of focus. I start with a strong sense of purpose, but before long, I catch myself preoccupied with lesser things, things that I was never meant to focus on. I get sidetracked with my own agenda and tend to forget what my life was really all about. My vision for my life is easily blurred. Helen Keller has a famous quote: "Worse than being blind would be to be able to see but not have any vision."

THE LIFE THAT thrives hinges only on the understanding that Christ is our all in all.

Do you need clear vision for your life?

If Paul knew one thing, it was vision. He knew what it meant to be intensely focused on knowing Jesus Christ as Lord with undisputed and undivided devotion. Paul was a man who looked on his singleness as a blessing for one reason only: the opportunity to offer his life in absolute devotion to the Savior who had delivered Paul, the chief of all sinners, from an eternity in hell.

And Paul thrived. Boy, did he thrive. No matter where life found Paul—in prison, in the church, on a journey, in a boat—this man understood that location was simply a place, and that the life that thrives hinges only on the understanding that Christ is our all in all.

But maybe you're not trying to be some super-Christian like Paul. You'd be happy with just average. Unfortunately, average is not an option with Christ. The brand of Christianity you're looking for is not on the menu. In Matthew 13:44, here's what Christ said about your walk with Him: "The kingdom of heaven is like treasure hidden in a field, which a man found and covered up. Then in his joy he goes and sells all that he has and buys that field."

Not dramatic enough for you? Try Luke 9:62: "Jesus said to him, 'No one who puts his hand to the plow and looks back is fit for the kingdom of God.'"

Luke 9:23–24 closely resembles 9:62: "If anyone would come after me, let him deny himself and take up his cross daily and follow me. For whoever would save his life will lose it, but whoever loses his life for my sake will save it."

Christ's call for you, regardless of your marital status, is straightforward. His is a call that demands your absolute surrender in every area of your life. You cannot selectively choose which parts of Christianity meet with your approval and which you will postpone until you're retired and have more time. Christ demands your undivided devotion today.

The blessing that you have as a single Christian is that you can pursue this undivided devotion with more focus and more energy than the married person. That's because as a single Christian, you've been freed from the anxiety of always trying to please your husband, and the anxiety that married life and a family bring along with it.

In other words, your entire purpose and goal, single Christian, if you call yourself a follower of Jesus Christ, is to be utterly and completely devoted to the Lord.

Instead of undivided devotion, many single Christians accumulate clutter that blurs and diminishes the vision. Instead of a pure love for the Lord, lesser loves creep in. Instead of a life that thrives in intimacy with the Lord, many single Christians feel a greater sense of isolation and separation from God.

So ask yourself: What stands in the way of my undivided

devotion for the Lord, and what does undivided devotion to the Lord look like? Let's start first by talking about the number one greatest competitor to your undivided devotion to the Lord.

THE #1 GREATEST COMPETITOR
FOR YOUR UNDIVIDED DEVOTION

I'm a huge Green Bay Packers fan, and though the Packers have many rivals, when it comes to the NFL and true rivalries, the Packers really have just one big enemy. If you haven't guessed it by now, it's the Chicago Bears. It doesn't matter that I live in Chicago and love the city of Chicago. When it comes to football, I cannot love both the Packers and the Bears. I always choose the Packers.

We're supposed to be talking about undivided devotion to the Lord, not football; yet the principle is the same. When it comes to loving God, the Bible tells us that there is one main and greatest competitor for that love. It's in Matthew 6:24: "No one can serve two masters, for either he will hate the one and love the other, or he will be devoted to the one and despise the other. You cannot serve God and money."

Bam. That's it. If you love money, you cannot love God. If you love God, you cannot love money. It doesn't get much easier to understand.

The first real paycheck I ever received was right after I graduated from medical school. I had just moved to Houston, and I made $32,000 that first year of my residency. I thought I was in heaven. I remember getting my first real paycheck, writing out my tithe check, and then going to the grocery store for some food. In the checkout line, I splurged and bought two things to celebrate: a copy of *People* magazine and a bouquet of cheap flowers.

I had never felt so rich. I had never felt so happy.

Today I make well over that amount of money, and can't believe that I ever survived on that first paycheck.

What I'm trying to say is that the issue of money is not about rich people and poor people. Money is an issue of the heart. You are either eternity minded, or earthly minded. You are either growing your kingdom or God's kingdom.

IF YOU LOVE money, you cannot love God. If you love God, you cannot love money.

So when it comes to your undivided devotion to the Lord, the greatest competitor for your focus on the Lord is money. Why is that such a big deal for the single Christian?

I have observed single Christians for some time now and find that they roughly fall into one of three categories:

1. The ones who don't make much money
2. The ones who make enough money and just *think* they don't make enough money
3. The ones who make enough money and *know* they make enough money

When you figure out which category you're in, start reading again.

God doesn't care how much money you make and frankly, neither do I. What God *does* care about is what you're doing with the money you do have. He also cares about where He falls in your personal organizational chart.

You may be so worried about your finances that you've picked up an extra job and have no time left for God. You may be so worried about saving more money that you've stopped giving faithfully. Or you may be so broke that you can't ever do anything for God; you can't even drive yourself to church, because you don't have enough money for gas.

Stop telling yourself your life would be easier if you were married. That's hogwash. You'd simply have more bills or different bills.

When your devotion to God becomes complete and undivided, money fades into the background. When God is your primary focus, you start seeing Him as your provider. The resources He gives you—whether a little or a lot—become simply tools toward further building His kingdom and accumulating a treasure in heaven.

STOP TELLING yourself your life would be easier if you were married.

I think about the great men and women of God who have had the most influence in the church. The majority of them were dirt broke, but rested secure in their undivided devotion to the Lord and saw God provide for every one of their needs.

When it comes to your wallet, who is in control: your God, or your bank? Have you accumulated so much debt in your attempt to numb your pain with material possessions that you've paralyzed yourself and can't serve the Lord?

Nothing blocks your ability to thrive like a heart that is captured by the love of money. When it comes to devotion, it's either God or money. Which will it be? You choose.

Money may be the primary competitor for undivided devotion to the Lord, but I can think of at least two other competitors for your focus. Let's talk about them next.

YOURSELF AS COMPETITION FOR YOUR UNDIVIDED DEVOTION TO GOD

If you've ever watched a photo shoot, you notice that nobody pays attention to the man behind the camera. The focus is instead on the famous person being photographed. Every single Christian is supposed to make God famous. You're supposed to hide behind the camera, trying to capture the best picture possible of Him. If you're like me, you find yourself tangled up and switching places with Him instead. You catch yourself yelling for the world to look at you—"Watch me! Watch me!"—as you clamor for attention.

The problem is that if you're a follower of Jesus Christ, your life is not about you. It's about Him. It's about making His name great. It's about confessing that He is the One worth watching. What are you doing in your life to make God great? When people look at you, do they see you or do they see God in you?

I can usually tell when I've made myself the center of attention, because I get upset when others don't give me the credit I feel I deserve. When that happens, I typically have to realign my focus and put the camera back on Jesus.

The Christian whose focus is on Jesus Christ is untouchable. If you don't get praise for a job well done, you're okay with it because you were doing it for God in the first place. When you get passed up for a promotion, you don't get riled up, because you trust God's sovereignty as you give Him your undivided devotion.

Life is good when Christ is at the center of it.

DISTRACTIONS AS COMPETITION FOR YOUR UNDIVIDED DEVOTION TO GOD

Did you know that the average person spends forty-nine minutes per day managing email? And that the average number of emails people receive a day is about seventy-five?[19] That's crazy.

Whether or not you are guilty of the same, the reality is that many single Christians are living their lives with spiritual ADD. You want to have undivided devotion to God, but you become easily distracted from it. You flutter around without ever really deepening your roots with the Lord, and pretty soon, you find that you can barely see the goal you set out toward when you first began your walk with Christ.

The opposite of spiritual ADD would be the example of my dad. He was one of those old-fashioned plastic surgeons. He lived and breathed plastic surgery. If you asked him what he did for fun, he looked at you with a blank stare as if you'd just asked the dumbest question in the world. If you caught him reading anything, it was usually a journal on plastic surgery. My dad had one love during his professional life—the love of plastic surgery. My father is the most amazing father in the world, but he's also a great example of undistracted and undivided devotion.

Are you easily distracted in your walk with the Lord? Do you find yourself divided in your love for Him? Are you trying to split your attention between hobbies and relationships and goals, leaving little time for the Savior? You will not thrive as a single Christian as long as your love is divided.

UNDIVIDED DEVOTION for God doesn't happen overnight. You must plan for it to happen.

Remember back when you first came to Christ? Your love was burning hot. Now you find your love for Christ has become lukewarm. In Revelation 2:4–5, Christ gives us the treatment for a lukewarm love. He says this: "Repent, and do the works you did at first" (verse 5).

Do you remember those works you used to do that secured your undivided devotion to the Lord? Why don't I review them for you.

WHAT DOES UNDIVIDED DEVOTION TO THE LORD LOOK LIKE?

Paul's instruction to the single Christian in 1 Corinthians 7:35 is for you to secure your undivided devotion to the Lord. What does that mean? What does that look like? The idea of undivided devotion is not some Kumbaya-singing, hand-holding, warm, fuzzy feeling that you used to get at junior high camp while throwing sticks in the fire. Undivided devotion for God doesn't happen overnight. It is intentional and specific. You must plan for it to happen.

Fortunately, God's Word helps us out when it comes to figuring out what devotion to the Lord looks like. I looked up every verse in the Bible that references devotion and found four areas in your life that require your devotion and promote your closer walk with the Lord.

1. Devotion to the Scriptures

The concept of being devoted to Scriptures shows up several times in the New Testament. It's no surprise that in order to know God more and to be more devoted to Him, the single Christian must study the Scriptures and know them. This is sometimes easier said than done.

I spent the bulk of my teen years struggling with my daily quiet time with the Lord. I wanted to have it, but I seemed to constantly fail in it. I would make a decision to read my Bible daily, do it for a week, and then fall off the wagon. I honestly didn't think I would ever get it down.

The year I started medical school, I was challenged to exercise daily in order to stay mentally and physically healthy. Since I was also a follower of Jesus Christ, and being the brainiac that you have come to know and love, I put two and two together and figured this would be a great time for me to get spiritually healthy as well. I then committed myself to a regular daily Bible-reading time in order to ensure my spiritual health. Right around that time, I heard that it takes twenty-one days to develop a habit. I believed it. I got a calendar out and literally crossed off days until I hit the twenty-first day and found that I had developed two new habits in my life: I ran and I read my Bible daily.

Twenty years and several injuries later, I'm an occasional runner, but I'm still reading my Bible daily and growing in my devotion to the Lord.

Nobody is born with an encyclopedic knowledge of God's Word. Isaiah 28:13 says that the word of the Lord is learned "precept upon precept . . . line upon line," here a little, there a little. So stop comparing yourself to your pastor or your mother, and start reading God's Word today. You will find that as you grow in your knowledge of God's Word, your devotion for God will grow too.

2. Devotion to Prayer

Reading the Bible is how Christians listen to God's voice in their life, but prayer is how Christians speak to God. We have confidence to pray because of the blood of Jesus Christ who made a way for us to God the Father. That's an incredible privilege and one that most Christians do not take advantage of.

THE LONGER I live, the more I see that all the strategy and all the methods in the world will not take me where prayer will.

When Paul tells the single Christian to secure undivided devotion to the Lord, one of the ways that you can do that is through prayer. Your singleness gives you more time and a greater ability to focus and develop a strong prayer life.

The more I pray and see God answer my requests, the more it hits me how little I pray. The longer I live, the more I see that all the strategy and all the methods in the world will not take me where prayer will. If you find your intimacy with the Lord lacking, perhaps you need to pray more.

3. Devotion to Good Works and Urgent Needs

Titus 3:14 says this: "And let our people learn to devote themselves to good works, so as to help cases of urgent need, and not be unfruitful."

This is a book about thriving. If you want to be fruitful and thrive, start devoting yourself to good works. As a single Christian, you are perfectly positioned to help with urgent needs. Most of you don't have kids to pick up from soccer practice (I'm not rubbing this in; I'm just stating a fact). You don't have to cook dinner for your husband. You are free to devote yourself to other people. If you're a single mother, your time is likely more limited; but God will surprise you in the ways you can show your devotion to Him through your good works.

4. Devotion to the Church

I doubt any group of Christians was as devoted to the Lord as the early church was in Acts 2. They had just witnessed Pentecost and were overflowing with the Holy Spirit. The very next snapshot of the early church is in Acts 2:42–

47. In this passage, we're told that the early Christians were devoted "to the apostles' teaching and the fellowship, to the breaking of bread and the prayers" (verse 42).

In other words, the early Christians, right after their filling with the Holy Spirit, understood that devotion to the Lord really meant devotion to His church.

If you're single, you are equipped like no other for devotion to the church. Sadly, many single Christians have negative feelings when it comes to the local church. Some have been hurt by the church. Others have given in to consumerism when it comes to serving the local church. Still others have a long list of dos and don'ts when it comes to serving in the church. They are afraid to roll up their sleeves and work for Christ. They are content to just sit on the bleachers and observe everybody else trying to do God's work.

It's time you get in the game. As you pour your life out for others and for Christ, you will deepen your walk with Christ in ways you never thought possible. Your intimacy with the Lord will grow in direct proportion to your work for Christ. Try it and see for yourself.

A FINAL ILLUSTRATION

I love this story from a news article about Pavarotti, the famous opera singer, who best illustrates what undivided devotion is.

When I was a boy, my father, a baker, introduced me to the wonders of song. He urged me to work very hard to develop my voice. Arrigo Pola, a professional tenor in my hometown of Modena, Italy, took me as a pupil. I also enrolled in a teachers college. On graduating, I asked my father, "Shall I be a teacher or a singer?"

"Luciano," my father replied, "if you try to sit on two chairs, you will fall between them. For life, you must choose one chair." I chose one. It took seven years of study and frustration before I made my first professional appearance. It took another seven to reach the Metropolitan Opera. And now I think whether it's laying bricks, writing a book—whatever we choose—we should give ourselves to it. Commitment, that's the key. Choose one chair.[20]

Every single Christian must make the same choice. Which chair will you choose? Will you embrace a life of undivided devotion to the Lord, or will you live for yourself?

Remember that "the gate is narrow and the way is hard that leads to life, and those who find it are few" (Matthew 7:14). I pray you are one of the few who find it.

PART 3

Four Obstacles to Overcome

7

Me, Myself, and I:
Defeating Self-Pity

I have a talent that few people know about. I can go from happy-go-lucky to pity-party faster than a race car can go from zero to sixty.

Yes, I'm an expert in self-pity, I guess you can call me a professional, of sorts, which makes me the perfect person to tell you about the first obstacle that you need to overcome in order to thrive as a single Christian.

Self-pity. It's a human condition. It's a bit of a curse, a definite downer, and until you learn to recognize it in your life and allow God to defeat it, you will remain miserable.

I like this quote from John Gardner on self-pity: "Self-pity is easily the most destructive of the non-pharmaceutical narcotics; it is addictive, gives momentary pleasure and separates the victim from reality."[21]

Too many Christians are held captive by the toxic emotion of self-pity. Too many Christians have found themselves wounded on the sidelines of life, waiting to be picked up and tended to, unable to overcome this seemingly insurmountable mountain.

I remember the first time I felt the weight of self-pity as a single Christian. I had just moved to a new town to start my fellowship in pediatric emergency medicine. It was the summer after I had ended an engagement to a wonderful young man who simply wasn't the one. I like to add that I broke off the engagement just two weeks before the wedding to make it a little more dramatic, but the breakup wasn't as Kardashian-worthy as I'd like to think. One day I was engaged, and the next day I wasn't. When most people hear about my story, they often comment on my courage but also assume that the event had ripped my heart to shreds. The truth is far different than that.

The truth is that I had fallen in love with someone else, my best friend of ten years.

Unfortunately, I'm a late bloomer in every way, and by the time I finally figured out what others had known for years, I was engaged to someone else, and two weeks away from my wedding day. Most of you are much smarter than I am, so you know that life is not a Hollywood movie, and I didn't get the happy ending I thought I would. By the time I woke up to the fallen state of my heart, my best friend had moved so far down a different road that there was no way I'd ever catch up.

By the time I had settled into my new apartment, in my new town, to start a new venture in pediatric emergency medicine, I was ripe for the taking. I was alone, depressed, and confused. Not only was my dream of happily-ever-after destroyed, but I had lost my best friend all in one fell swoop. That summer, the movie *My Best Friend's Wedding* came out, and I tortured myself in the theater while quietly watching my life play out on the big screen, feeling myself fall just a little bit deeper into the pit of self-pity that I had already dug for myself.

THE TRUTH IS that I had fallen in love with someone else, my best friend of ten years.

I had a two-bedroom apartment by the beach at that time. I moved into one room, and self-pity moved into the other.

I vividly recall coming home after a long shift in the ER and simply sitting in the middle of my living room, waiting for the sun to set, too depressed to turn the lights on. It all sounds very "Meryl Streep" as I now write it, but I suppose I do like my share of drama. My only company during those nights was the sounds of the night, the chirping of crickets in the man-made pond outside my apartment and in my head saying things like, *You asked for this. If only you hadn't gotten engaged. Where's God now? I thought you said God was the One who told you to end the engagement? Huh? You deserve better than this. Nothing's ever gonna change for you. Prayer? What good did prayer do for you last year, or the year before? If this is love, are you sure you want it? Where is God right now? I bet He's forgotten all about you. If He cared about you, you wouldn't be in this mess.*

Are you familiar with this conversation? You may have had a similar version of it at some point in your life. You probably know that it doesn't take long for self-pity to turn to defeat and then to despair while Satan dances around in glee, watching our hearts bleed slowly and steadily while our faith deconstructs one little brick at a time.

Self-pity is a toxic emotion that must be defeated if you intend to thrive. Let me give you a definition for self-pity. Self-pity is a self-indulgent attitude about your own difficulties and circumstances. Ironically, though self-pity seems to be the cry of the weak, it is actually rooted in pride. Listen to what John Piper says about self-pity:

> The nature and depth of human pride are illuminated by comparing boasting with self-pity. Both are manifestations of pride. Boasting is the response of pride to success. Self-pity is the response of pride to suffering. Boasting says, "I deserve admiration because I have achieved so much." Self-pity says, "I deserve admiration because I have sacrificed so much." Boasting is the voice of pride in the heart of the strong. Self-pity is the voice of pride in the heart of the weak. Boasting sounds self-sufficient. Self-pity sounds self-sacrificing. The reason self-pity does not look like pride is that it appears to be needy. But the need arises from a wounded ego, and the desire of the self-pitying is not really for others to see them as helpless, but as heroes. The need self-pity feels does not come from a sense of unworthiness, but from a sense of unrecognized worthiness. It is the response of un-applauded pride.[22]

In Jeremiah 17:9 God says that "the heart is deceitful above all things, and desperately sick; who can understand it?" How true His Word is. My own heart deceived me in the darkness of my living room, convincing me that I was the victim, and that God had abandoned me, that life was unfair, when all along I was sinking in the pit of my own pride.

I eventually overcame the obstacle of self-pity. Later on in this chapter, I'll tell you how. Once in a while, I still have a tendency to visit the pit of self-pity for old times' sake, but God's mercy never lets me stay there for too long. Let me identify some common signs that you may be struggling with self-pity.

SIGNS AND SYMPTOMS OF SELF-PITY

As an ER doctor, I've learned that the secret to any correct diagnosis is to carefully listen to the patient's presenting symptoms. In the case of self-pity, I'd like to give you these common signs and symptoms that may indicate you struggle with self-pity:

1. You Believe You've Been Given Less Than You Deserve

When you consider your life, you can't help but wonder why you've been shortchanged by God. You tell yourself that you've done your part. You've tried to maintain your purity. You're still a virgin. You've read your Bible and prayed. You even taught VBS that one year. But if you're honest with yourself, you've come to the point where you even doubt God's existence. You're not sure prayer really works at all. You tried praying, and nothing happened. If you were God, you'd see that no one deserves the mess you've been given.

IRONICALLY, though self-pity seems to be the cry of the weak, it is actually rooted in pride. Even though Christians say that they believe God has given them more than they deserve in this life, many secretly hang on to the notion that when it comes to their daily life, they deserve just a little bit more than God has given them.

If you're familiar with the story of the prodigal son, you can't help but feel just a little bit like the big brother did. You can't help but feel that you've done all the work for all these years, and that you deserve more. Pretty soon your thinking starts seeping into your heart until the gap between yourself and the Lord becomes too wide to ever overcome.

If you're walking around with the idea that you deserve more than you've been given, watch out for self-pity in your heart.

2. You've Been Given Less Than Others Have Been Given

In this case, you not only feel like you deserve more than you've been given, but you wonder why God has dealt everyone else a better deal. It's easy to magnify other people's lives and assume that God has given them preferential treatment. When I lost my best friend, I couldn't understand why God had chosen to reward his new wife instead, while I sat alone in my dark apartment. Wasn't I the one who had given my life to the Lord as a teenager while she'd just recently become a follower of Jesus Christ? How fair was that?

In today's world, you can thank Facebook for the shove down the pit of self-pity that it gives you. Did you know that a recent study found that Facebook envy can actually make you miserable? The study showed that "one in three people felt worse after visiting the site and more dissatisfied with their lives, while people who browsed without contributing were affected the most."[23] Those aren't good numbers if you're prone to comparing yourself with others. Nothing invites self-pity over like a cursory comparison of your life to your Facebook friends' lives and finding yourself on the short end of the stick. You may know in your head that Facebook is the prettier, more fun, perfect version of everyone's life, but your heart still can't help silently questioning God's fairness in your life.

It's even worse if your ex (fiancé, husband, boyfriend) is on Facebook. Now you get to check up on the progress he's made in his life while you struggle to meet your day-to-day challenges. If that's you, let me get a head start on the solution to your problem and tell it to you right now: get rid of Facebook. The cycle will never end. There will always be someone prettier, smarter, richer, or better than you are. God's purpose for your life is uniquely yours. Until you stop looking at the greener grass on the other side, you will remain on the losing side of self-pity.

3. You've Been Given Nothing Good

I get in seasons in my life when my hair has too much static and my face is too pale, and I just feel really sorry for myself. I'm single, dateless, and I have love handles. It's those days when nothing you wear looks good. I daydream about what my life would have been like had I simply gotten married the first time I was engaged, and ended up living in East Texas. Then I pinch myself. Oh boy. Someone speak truth into my life right now! What would a girl like me do in East Texas?

If you know anything about self-pity, you know that when you have it, you dread the moment someone asks you to point out the "good things" in your life. Good things? What good things? There's nothing good in my life! When I hit those seasons of negativity, it's best to stay out of the way and tell me to stop talking!

4. You're Convinced Things Will Never Get Better

You'll never go out on a date again. You'll never pay off the debt you have. You'll always live in your dingy little apartment. You'll never be as pretty as you were five years ago. Oh, and you'll never have sex in this lifetime and there won't be sex in heaven, so you're double-doomed.

You can keep on adding to your list, but self-pity brings with it the idea that your life will never get better than it currently is. You convince yourself that you will never be happy again. You are at a dead-end road, and good luck getting back on the road to joy.

You're not the only one who has been tempted to believe this lie. The Israelites believed this lie before they entered the Promised Land. Gideon believed this lie before God used him to deliver Israel. Naomi believed this lie before God brought Boaz to deliver her and Ruth. I could go on and on with biblical examples, but in each case, things did get better, and they will in your life too.

If you're struggling with self-pity right now, I hope you won't stay there long.

5. You're Resigned to God's Will in Your Life

Lastly, you know you've sunk in self-pity if you've simply resigned yourself to God's will. You're too polite or afraid to question God. Instead, you quietly go along with His plans, but wonder about His wisdom in them. You don't trust God much anymore, but you know better than to question Him. You may think you're being obedient, but the chip on your shoulder that is growing with each passing day contradicts your actions.

> ## YOU KNOW you've sunk in self-pity if you've simply resigned yourself to God's will.

While you may think you're doing God's will, this resigned attitude is still rooted in self-pity. You secretly feel like the victim in God's master plan. Yet God's character is so far from this detached, punishing God. He is a loving God, and He is ever-faithful. He isn't looking for your resigned obedience, but for your willful surrender. He loves you.

But I'm getting ahead of myself. Before we talk about ways to overcome self-pity, I want to give you some common triggers of self-pity. Watch for them and learn to avoid them.

TRIGGERS OF SELF-PITY

When I think back to those months spent in my dark apartment feeling sorry for myself, I can't believe how predictable my spiral down into self-pity was. I'm surprised I didn't see it coming. When I look back to those days, I see four obvious triggers that always landed me in the pit of self-pity. Here they are:

1. Unchecked Introspection

I've always been a bit on the analytical side and given to introspection. I like to process things at length. I mull things over in my mind until they're mush, and I strive to come up with the right solution to whatever problem I'm dealing with. I also grew up encouraged to journal and regularly evaluate my life against God's Word. Introspection may be fine and dandy when done under the protection of God's Word and the control of the Holy Spirit, but left unchecked, it will lead you down the pit of self-pity faster than you can blink.

Think about the times you've tried to have your quiet time with the Lord, and thirty minutes later you haven't even opened your Bible but have a list of complaints about your life written in your journal. It's never good.

You must get in the habit of carefully guarding your mind and sieving every thought through the filter of God's Word. If you find yourself daydreaming about me and myself and I, and what should have been or what could have been in your life, I can tell you where you're headed. It may be time to stop and turn around.

As a single Christian, your challenge is even greater because you may not have the advantage of having someone to check your thoughts and gently nudge you back in the right direction, leaving you alone and unchecked. Thinking back on my time as a newcomer in a new city without any friends or social network, I was particularly heady material for self-pity. Learn from my experience and surround yourself with godly influences in your life. You'll be glad you did.

2. Unfounded Conclusions

The mind is an interesting organ. It can take you places you never intended to go. You may not know yourself to be a novelist, but you've probably written more fiction works about your life while in the dark pit of self-pity than you care to admit.

Unfortunately, we do this all the time. Just yesterday I received an email from a friend who was hurt because I hadn't invited her to a luncheon I went to. She felt that I purposefully left her out because of some grudge I was carrying. I responded back to the friend and explained that I hadn't even realized that I had excluded her and that the invitation hadn't been mine to extend, and everything turned out fine between us. To my friend's credit, she had come to me with her concerns, but I am still amazed at the brain's ability to build unfounded conclusions based on some untrue, meager facts we hear. She's not alone. I do the same thing all the time, and I bet you do too.

We see a party on Facebook and become convinced of some conspiracy theory against us, leaving us out. You get the point. Satan takes great joy in throwing little tidbits our way to help us develop these lies that turn us against the Lord. Be careful when you catch yourself making unfounded conclusions about other people's lives. Nothing could be further from the truth, and nothing could more sneakily poison your soul.

3. Unrealistic Expectations

My eight-year-old nephew looked forward to his birthday for a whole month. We heard about it daily. When the day finally arrived, it was a major letdown. School had ended the month before, so he couldn't celebrate with his friends. It rained on his birthday. Nothing turned out like he thought it would. It was my nephew's first lesson in disappointed expectations; and the sooner he learns to deal with it, the better off he'll be as an adult. Wow. That's harsh. But you know it's true.

I FULLY EXPECTED God to bend Himself backward to make my plans happen and was massively disappointed when He did not.

Unfortunately, we all struggle with unrealistic expectations about our lives. They tend to creep up on us on special events and holidays. The problem with unrealistic expectations is that they are usually centered on me, myself, and I. Our expectations attempt to use God to meet our personal needs rather than focus on God as our only expectation. When I sat in my dark living room, I thought of God a lot. I even prayed a lot. I hung on to my expectations where my best friend would finally see the light and come chasing after me, and sweep me off my feet, and my life would still end up with my version of my "happily ever after." I fully expected God to bend Himself backward to make my plans happen and was massively disappointed when He did not.

But today, by God's grace, I'm happy to tell you that God had far better plans for my life and for my best friend and his wife. I could not have foreseen the wisdom and love of God's plans. His plans have allowed me to thrive in my life in a way I never thought possible.

4. Unplanned Free Time

The last trigger to self-pity is the trigger of unplanned free time. It's Friday night and you're home alone. You have nothing to do. You start flipping through the television and come across a romantic comedy you've already seen a dozen times. Two hours and a pint of ice cream later, you're tearful and sad. You can't understand why everyone else gets a happy ending while you're rotting away in your basement, wasting the best years of your life. You blame yourself, you blame your ex, you blame your parents, and you finally blame God. Doesn't He care about you? If He did, wouldn't He do something about it? Next thing you know, not only are you mad at the world and at God, but you take out your anger by throwing self-control out the window. If you're prone to the sins of the flesh, you revert to your favorite vice for comfort. If you're a binge eater, you get yourself a second pint of ice cream. You get the gist, and it's ugly.

Single Christians who work hard all week look forward to nights alone when they can simply relax. I've found that those are the very nights that Satan will use to defeat you. There may be other key nights for you to watch out for, like Valentine's Day, or the anniversary of your engagement or your wedding day. On those difficult days, don't allow yourself unplanned free time. Instead, surround yourself with godly friends and make an active plan to stop self-pity the moment it rears its ugly head.

I should know. I've been beaten down by self-pity far too many times.

DEFEATING SELF-PITY

My pastor, James MacDonald, has a great saying about God's love. He often tells his congregation, "God's love is not a pampering love, it's a perfecting love."

I never fully understood what he meant until the summer after my first big breakup. At first I wouldn't even turn the lights on when I came home from work. I took secret joy in the darkness. It became a salve for my wounded heart. Outwardly I still did the things I was supposed to do. I went to work. I went to church. I was too well-trained to skip church, but I made sure I didn't *talk* to anyone at church. I was happy in my misery.

One day it was raining particularly hard when I heard a knock on my door. *Odd*, I thought. I don't know anyone in this neck of the woods, and I knew not to open the door to strangers. The knock persisted. It was too late for me to turn off the lights and act like I wasn't home, so I gingerly got up and checked the peephole.

What I saw amazed me. There were two older ladies and a man. I'd never seen them before, but what threat could two little old ladies be to me? I was already too beaten down by my own self. I opened the door, perplexed.

"Are you Lina Aaabuujaamara?" one of the ladies cheerfully asked.

"Um . . . yes? And who are you?"

"We're visiting you from the church. We just wanted to see how you were settling in," she sang back, undaunted.

Huh? I confess I was a bit taken aback. I tend to be a little intimidating in person, but this woman was unfazed. She had an agenda for the evening, and it included me.

I couldn't believe it. I couldn't believe that anyone would drive forty-five minutes in the rain simply to check up on me. The visitors had no idea what I had been going through.

But God knew.

The visitors had no idea that I was in a pit too deep to get out of on my own.

But God knew.

IT DIDN'T MATTER how dark my pit had become, the darkness was simply not dark to God.

There is a verse in Isaiah 49:15–16 that goes like this: "Can a woman forget her nursing child, that she should have no compassion on the son of her womb? Even these may forget, yet I will not forget you. Behold, I have engraved you on the palms of my hands; your walls are continually before me." What I hadn't taken into account, deep in the pit of my self-induced and self-focused despair, was that several years before, when I was just a child, I had been adopted by the King of kings. My name had been imprinted on His hands—forever.

I was His, for better or for worse. It didn't matter how dark my pit had become, the darkness was simply not dark to God. It didn't matter that I didn't know my way out of my pit, because God had just pulled me out of it.

The next morning, I was ready to hear God's voice again. I opened the Bible and landed in Isaiah 43. "When you pass through the waters, I will be with you; and through the rivers, they shall not overwhelm you. . . . Because you are precious in my eyes, and honored, and I love you" (verses 2, 4). God had just wrecked me with His love.

That fall, I made my way through the Minor Prophets and fell in love with my Savior all over again. What Satan had intended for destruction, God used for my good. That following year, I sensed God calling me to the ministry of teaching the Bible to women. It would take another decade for that story to fully play out, but God had plucked me out of the pit and set my feet on a rock.

You may be in the pit of self-pity as you read my story. The same God who pulled me out of my pit is pulling you out of yours. Life as a single Christian is not easy. The temptation to give up on God is too great. It's easy to feel forgotten and alone in a world of independence and greater isolation than ever. But God is closer to you than you think.

I'd like to end this chapter by giving you three principles I learned about God from my time with self-pity. Though I kicked self-pity out of my home that year, I find that every once in a while, I have to revisit these principles to avoid landing in the same pit. I hope you will find them helpful too.

1. God Can Handle Your Pain

King David understood this principle like no other. In Psalm 56:8 he said, "You have kept count of my tossings; put my tears in your bottle. Are they not in your book?" And in Psalm 62:8 he said, "Pour out your heart before him; God is a refuge for us."

I'm not sure why I believed the lie that I could only come to God with my church clothes on, that He somehow couldn't handle my mess. I couldn't have been more wrong. I need God the most when I'm hurting and dirty and desperate for help. That's when He wants me to run into His arms. He's not afraid of my questions or yours. He loves you. He can handle your pain if you'll just try Him.

2. God Will Give You the Answers You Need

The answers don't always come the moment you want them, but they are sure to come. They say that time heals all wounds. As a cynic, I've always doubted the truth of that statement, but as a doctor I've found it to be true. Every wound that doesn't kill you will eventually heal. Oh, it may leave a scar, but the scar is a reminder of where you've been. The scar makes the man, or the woman in my case.

Though my life is plenty filled with scars, God has proven Himself faithful to me again and again. He has given me the answers in His Word when I've looked for them there. He has given me the answers through His people when I've asked for them there. He has given me the answers in the moments when I've patiently waited for Him to do so. And I know He'll do the same for you.

3. God Has a Better Plan Than You Can Imagine

Everybody loves Jeremiah 29:11. If you're not familiar with it, you're going to love it too. It says, "For I know the plans I have for you, declares the Lord, plans for welfare and not for evil, to give you a future and a hope." Isn't it great?

Personally, I have two other favorite verses. The first is my life verse. Every Christian ought to have one. Mine is Philippians 1:6, which says, "And I am sure of this, that he who began a good work in you will bring it to completion at the day of Jesus Christ."

The other verse is an old standby that goes like this: "And we know that for those who love God all things work together for good, for those who are called according to his purpose" (Romans 8:28).

I share these verses to remind you that God's plan for your life is good. He wants you to thrive. He wants to pour His favor on you. In order for Him to do so, you must get to the place where you can receive it. Ask Him to forgive you for the sinful conclusions you've had about Him and for misjudging His character. Ask Him to forgive you for the sinful actions you've turned to for comfort. As you repent and turn to Him, you'll see that His plans are far better than you can imagine. He never disappoints His children.

4. God Will Someday Use Your Pain for His Glory

When I went through my time in the darkness, I never imagined that one day I'd be writing my story for you to read and perhaps be encouraged by. Honestly, given a choice, I would prefer never to go back to that time in my life again. But for God to use me in ministry, He first needed to break me. I tend to be extremely strong and self-dependent. It would have never crossed my mind to be heartbroken over a guy. Yet God in His wisdom saw my life when as yet my days were not formed. He is that wise and that good. The more I know Him, the more I trust Him.

The life that thrives is the life that is fully surrendered to the Lord. The life that thrives trusts that today's pain will be used for God's glory tomorrow.

I don't know about you, but I'm through with self-pity. I think we're ready to move on to the next obstacle that every single Christian must overcome in order to thrive. Are you ready for it?

8

Soul Killer:
Uprooting Bitterness

L ove never goes as planned.

If you've watched enough romantic comedies and read enough books, you have probably subliminally acquired the notion that love is your right, and that without it you will never be happy.

But if you've lived long enough, you realize that some people never find the big love. Others find it and lose it all too soon. Still others find it, marry it, only to find out that it makes funny noises at night and doesn't do the dishes. Sooner or later, you will find yourself disillusioned by love.

Life doesn't always follow a Hollywood script. You've already heard my sad tale, and you haven't even heard the other half of it.

I've been engaged twice. After the first engagement, my fiancé had a nervous breakdown, and the second time, I did. I am exaggerating on both accounts, but the reality is that by the time any relationship—with its hope for a "happily ever after"—ends, it can certainly feel like you're having a nervous breakdown.

While the first broken engagement left me with a shattered heart, the second one simply threatened to leave me bitter. Let me tell you about it.

I finished my fellowship in pediatric emergency medicine and moved to Chicago. This was an exciting time in my life. I was through with my training after fourteen years of hard work and felt doubly blessed by God's calling me into ministry. I assumed the doors in Chicago would fly open with people begging for me to live out God's will for my life.

I assumed wrong.

I also assumed that since I'd done my time in brokenheartedness and datelessness, that I'd finally meet the perfect guy in Chicago and live happily ever after. It was finally going to be my time.

Again, I assumed wrong.

If you know anything about God's call on people's lives, it is not a cakewalk. It is a call that will utterly destroy every sense of self-sufficiency you may have and put you in a place where all you can say is "uncle."

It took the Lord six years to get me to cry "uncle." Those six years are a topic for another book, but I'll summarize them by saying that I was wrecked (not in the positive and hip way that everyone's using the word these days but seriously, truly wrecked) and ready for anything.

It was around that time that the Lord brought a wonderful young man into my life. And the angels in heaven lifted their hands and sang, as did my mother. This guy was perfect, on paper. He had everything a single Christian girl could want, on paper, but he simply wasn't the right one for me.

Of course you know my pattern by now. It took getting

engaged to finally recognize that this guy, as hard as I tried to force him to be, wasn't the one.

SOME PEOPLE never find the big love. Others find it and lose it all too soon. Still others find it, marry it, only to find out that it makes funny noises at night and doesn't do the dishes.

By God's grace the relationship disintegrated, this time several months before the supposed wedding, and I was back in square one—single and sad. But this time I'd also picked up a small bag along the way, the bag of bitterness.

How could God do this to me twice? How could that "Christian" guy fail to leave out that one minor detail about his life that would change everything for us? They say, "Fool me once, shame on you. Fool me twice, shame on me," but all I felt was anger at the guy, the God, the life that I had been so pitifully dealt. By now Facebook had been invented, so every sick aspect of my relationship was an open book for friend and foe to read, study, and analyze. (Warning to all single people out there: be careful what you share on Facebook. It always has a way of coming back to haunt you.)

Anyway, here I was, older but not wiser, wondering all over again where I went wrong.

We're talking about how to thrive in the single Christian life. Earlier in the book, we covered the five attitudes to embrace for the life that thrives. We are now discussing the four obstacles to overcome in order to thrive. In the last chapter we defeated self-pity, and now we're ready to move forward and uproot the bitterness that can so easily creep up in the single life.

The only place bitterness is allowed is in your morning coffee where black, no cream, and no sugar, is not only allowed but encouraged. Everywhere else, bitterness poisons the soul. It is often hard to admit, difficult to diagnose, and it is almost always destructive. It will steal your joy and poison your relationships, and it will absolutely prevent you from thriving.

Simply defined, bitterness is the feeling of anger, hurt, or resentment toward someone. It is typically a result of hurt caused by another person or a past experience in your life. It is directed at other people or sometimes toward God.

I think this well-known illustration captures the essence of bitterness extremely well:

One day, two monks were walking through the countryside. They were on their way to another village to help bring in the crops. As they walked, they spied an old woman sitting at the edge of a river. She was upset because there was no bridge, and she could not get across on her own. The first monk kindly offered, "We will carry you across if you would like." "Thank you," she said gratefully, accepting their help. So the two men joined hands, lifted her between them and carried her across the river. When they got to the other side, they set her down, and she went on her way.

After they had walked another mile or so, the second monk began to complain. "Look at my clothes," he said.

"They are filthy from carrying that woman across the river. And my back still hurts from lifting her. I can feel it getting stiff." The first monk just smiled and nodded his head.

A few more miles up the road, the second monk griped again, "My back is hurting me so badly, and it is all because we had to carry that silly woman across the river! I cannot go any farther because of the pain." The first monk looked down at his partner, now lying on the ground, moaning. "Have you wondered why I am not complaining?" he asked. "Your back hurts because you are still carrying the woman. But I set her down five miles ago."

One of the reasons you may not be thriving as a single Christian could be that you're just like that second monk, having a difficult time letting go of some baggage in your life. No matter how hard you've tried to move past your disappointments, you find yourself holding on to the pain of the past, even exalting it, and diligently nurturing your root of bitterness until it slowly threatens to destroy your whole life. Your only option for the freedom to thrive is to decisively yank the root of bitterness out of your life. Here's what the writer of the book of Hebrews says about bitterness in Hebrews 12:15: "See to it that no one fails to obtain the grace of God; that no 'root of bitterness' springs up and causes trouble, and by it many become defiled."

I'm not much of a gardener, but I try. I love to see a lush green yard and colorful flowers. Yet even my inexperienced eye knows that weeds kill plants and that the only way to get rid of them is to yank them out by their roots. To only remove the visible portion of the weed is a total waste of time.

THE ONLY PLACE bitterness is allowed is in your morning coffee where black, no cream, and no sugar, is not only allowed but encouraged.

In keeping with the biblical analogy of bitterness as a root in a garden, consider these observations about bitterness.

Bitterness Starts Small

Weeds typically start out really, really small, but left to themselves, they will take over your entire garden. Even though you may not see bitterness right away, God's Word doesn't lie. That small root of bitterness in your life, if allowed to spring up, will bring with it much trouble. If you don't deal with your anger toward God and others right away, time will not improve the situation. It will only make things worse.

Bitterness Grows Deep

Bitterness spreads wide, taking over your life, but it also grows deep, clutching your heart like a jellyfish's tentacles on your skin. To remove bitterness, you must be willing to do the dirty work (although it may not be as bad as peeing on your own leg to get the jellyfish off). You cannot approach it with a weak and halfhearted effort. It will take all of your strength to dig out the root of bitterness that has been slowly growing in your heart. If you've been harboring bitterness for years, the work will be harder and will demand more intentional and focused effort, but it will be necessary if you're looking for the life that thrives. This is serious, and often painful work, and demands a serious approach.

Bitterness Affects Many

In Hebrews 12:15, God warns us that if left unchecked, that root of bitterness will cause many to become defiled. You may already be seeing the effects that your bitterness has on the people in your life. Your bitterness will affect your children if you're a single mother with unresolved anger. Your bitterness will affect your friendships if you're a "never married" with a growing chip on your shoulder. Your bitterness will even affect your future relationships, God help you. This is no joking matter. You must take care of bitterness before the poison seeps over from your life to the lives of others.

Bitterness Will Bring You Down

Bitterness is bad. It will negatively affect everyone around you, but worst of all it will lead to your spiritual death. Let me explain where the concept of the root in the Hebrews verse comes from. If you go all the way back to Deuteronomy 29:18, you will find this verse: "Beware lest there be among you a man or woman or clan or tribe whose heart is turning away today from the Lord our God to go and serve the gods of those nations. Beware lest there be among you a root bearing poisonous and bitter fruit."

Do you see it? The root that bears poison will lead to bitter fruit that will rip your heart away from the Lord God and lead you to serve other gods. Make no mistake: bitterness is deadly. You cannot mess around with it. You must deal with it now.

SIGNS THAT YOU MAY BE BITTER

So here I was in my late thirties, confused, single, and bitter. At first I didn't recognize that the problem issue in my life was bitterness. If you'd asked me if I was bitter, I would have denied it. But I did know something was wrong. I was having a hard time praying, but couldn't quite put my finger on why I was so unhappy.

One day, I did the unthinkable. I broke into my second ex-fiancé's email. That's when I knew I had a serious problem.

Look—I never would have guessed I had a bitterness problem. Sure, I struggled with self-pity, and yes, I had some anger and self-control issues, but bitterness? Me? No way. My heart was pure gold. If you're thinking along those same lines, think again. Let me give you four common signs that reveal you have a bitter heart:

1. You Regularly Run "What If" Scenarios in Your Head

When my second engagement ended, I became plagued with "what if" scenarios. What if I hadn't gotten engaged the first time? What if I had asked the right questions the second time around? What if I had prayed more or sinned less? What if I hadn't pushed the boundaries in the physical aspect of our relationship?

You know the gig. You can't help yourself. You are sure that your life should have turned out differently if only_____ (you fill in the blank). You replay every minute of every situation and conversation. It doesn't even have to be about your love life. Maybe you're bitter at your parents and it's keeping you from thriving. You are convinced that if you had been born in a different home, your life would have turned out differently. If only your parents weren't so strict.

I WAS HAVING a hard time praying, but couldn't quite put my finger on why I was so unhappy.

The problem with "what if" scenarios is that all they do is simply fuel the anger you have toward the person involved. In my case, it was anger at my ex-fiancés. The more time I spent fantasizing over what should have been, the deeper the root of bitterness wrapped itself around my heart. In running "what if" scenarios in my head, I was also removing the God factor from my life. There are no "what ifs" when you're a child of God. Everything that happens in your life happens for a reason. If you're prone to "what ifs," you need to watch out for bitterness in your life.

2. You Regularly Check Up on Your Exes

I told you my big bad secret. It's like a disease that we can't keep ourselves from getting. You tell yourself you won't go there, but soon you find yourself on Facebook, Google, blogs, and any other site that will leak any information about the point of your anger. It could be years since your high school frenemy hurt you, but you still do your cursory check on her life via Google, Facebook, Twitter, and LinkedIn. You just need to know that he's still single and waiting for you, or divorced and hurting. You can't help but look at his girlfriend and tell yourself she's not as smart or as talented as you are. If this sounds familiar, you may be dealing with a small root of bitterness in your heart. Pull it out before it takes you out.

3. You Regularly Review Past Hurts Done to You

Nothing feels quite as good as getting together with friends and bashing the person who has hurt you. The more others agree with you, the more justified you feel. A guy I once dated had decided not to kiss me until we were married. I remember the day he changed his profile picture and put a new one up of himself and his new girlfriend kissing. Within sixty minutes, at least four of my friends had texted me to tell me. I spent the next week reviewing every hurt he'd ever committed against me.

By God's grace, I eventually figured out that I had a problem with bitterness and dealt with it. Maybe you need to deal with this kind of problem too.

4. You Regularly Have One-Sided Conversations with God about It

This one is my favorite. You tell yourself you're praying, but all you're really doing is having a one-sided conversation with God where your mouth is moving but nothing is happening. No wonder you don't feel God's presence in your life anymore. I've already told you in the last chapter that God can handle your pain, but this isn't about pain. What you're dealing with right here is anger and your unconfessed sin of unforgiveness.

I'll tell you how you know the conversation has switched from a one-way to a two-way conversation. It's when you finally hear God saying, "Let it go. Forgive him," and you do it. Are you willing to do it? You need to do it if you want a life that thrives.

LIES BITTERNESS BELIEVES

If you've identified the root of bitterness in your life, then I hope you're ready to uproot it by now. One of the ways I like to deal with heart issues is to first understand the lies behind my beliefs. When it comes to bitterness, here are three common lies I believed:

1. I Was Wronged by the Other Person

When I think of people who were wronged in life, my mind immediately goes to Joseph, whose brothers sold him as a slave to the Egyptians. I also think of David, who was almost killed by Saul despite all David had done for his nation. I think of the many prophets who told the truth and paid dearly for it, sometimes spending years in prison, being beaten, or being ridiculed for it. The examples in the Bible are endless, of people who did the right thing but were treated unjustly. How easy it could have been for someone like Joseph to become bitter.

Instead, Joseph made the astounding observation in Genesis 50:20: "As for you, you meant evil against me, but God meant it for good, to bring it about that many people should be kept alive, as they are today."

That's supernatural, and that's exactly the life you need in order to thrive. Joseph was indeed wronged. But the key to Joseph's success was that despite the wrong, he was able to see God's sovereign control over his life and circumstances.

Can you do the same?

2. I Was Wronged by God

It's hard to admit to anyone that you've felt wronged by God. But consider my life at the time of my second breakup. I had already gone through a hurt and survived it the Joseph way. I had also given my life to the Lord for ministry, was teaching Bible studies, going on mission trips, tithing regularly, and making strides in my thought life. If I could keep my end of the deal, wouldn't God?

It made no sense to me that this God would set me up that way, and humiliate me so publicly. A few hours after I ended my second engagement, I had to show up for my shift in the ER. I had been the talk of the ER with my upcoming nuptials, especially for a gal like me who had hardly ever dated and was an outspoken Christian. People had been so happy for me. That afternoon, I was embarrassed for myself, for God, and for my type of Christianity.

I felt as if God had let me down.

And I was wrong. I was misjudging God and ruining His character. I took no responsibility for my part in the wrong. I needed to repent, plain and simple.

For what it's worth, I'm happy to tell you that God's character endured my breakup, and so has my faith. By His grace, I rest securely in the loving arms of my Father. But we'll talk more about that in a bit.

3. I'll Never Get Over This

I never thought I'd get over the love of my life. I never thought I'd get over one broken engagement, let alone two. I never thought I'd get over my failures in life. I bet Samson never thought he'd get over his stupidity that night when he finally caved and gave up his hair secrets to Delilah. I bet David never felt he'd get over his sin with Bathsheba. And I bet Peter, at the foot of the cross, never thought he'd get over his own failure.

Left to ourselves, we'd all stay in the misery of our own bitterness over our own failures, our own pasts, and our own mistakes. Left to ourselves, every one of us would remain angry and hurt by another person, and sometimes rightfully so.

But that's not Christ's way. Colossians 3:13 says, "Forgiving each other; as the Lord has forgiven you, so you also must forgive."

Christ's way is to generously forgive the undeserving. I am astounded at God's mercy and forgiveness in my own life. I see Him still using me even when I know the darkness of my own heart. I see Him redeeming my mistakes and giving me more than I deserve, time and time again, and I'm amazed at the persistent and steadfast depth of His love for me.

I FELT AS if God had let me down.

If you're a child of God and are determined to obey Him, you will get over your anger and bitterness, but you've got to let go of a few things first.

THE WAY TO UPROOT BITTERNESS

I think we've established by now that bitterness is not good for the life that thrives. It doesn't matter if you're bitter at your brother, mother, father, boyfriend, or ex-husband; it's high time you move on in your life. In order to do so, you need to let go of these five things.

1. Let Go of Your Sin

I hope by now you've seen the sinful pattern of thinking in your own heart. You may have blamed God for not caring about you, or you may still be blaming your ex while ignoring your own sin in your past. Regardless, you cannot move forward in your relationship with the Lord until you confess your sin and turn from it.

The afternoon I caught myself breaking into my ex-fiancé's email account, I got a glimpse into the depth of my own bitterness. That day, I turned to the Lord in repentance and let go of my sin. I confessed to the Lord that I had doubted His sovereignty and His goodness to me. I confessed to the Lord that I had accused Him of mismanaging my life. I confessed my own sin of lust that had clouded my thinking, and I confessed my sin of people pleasing that strove to impress others with my perfectly self-righteous life. I had a long list to confess, but God was right there ready to forgive me. And He'll do the same for you.

2. Let Go of the Person

There is a great parable that Jesus told in Matthew 18:21–35. Peter had just asked Christ how often we ought to forgive each other. Peter, thinking he was being very gracious, threw in a generous number—seventy times seven times.

Wow, Peter, good for you, everyone must have thought. But Jesus didn't. Jesus thinks differently than we do.

He would then go on to tell His disciples the story of

a king and his servant. The servant owed the king a ton of money, like millions. The king graciously forgave him his debt. Later on, that same servant had a guy in his life who owed him nothing but a measly dollar (I'm paraphrasing, but you get the idea). The poor guy begged for mercy, but the first servant refuses. He sent the poor guy to prison.

Of course the king heard about it, as kings always do, and the day of reckoning came for the evil servant. The lesson is obvious, and Jesus summed it up with this reaction from the king: "You wicked servant! I forgave you all that debt because you pleaded with me. And should not you have had mercy on your fellow servant, as I had mercy on you?" (Matthew 18:32–33).

In case it's still not clear to you, let me rephrase it: you need to forgive the person who has wronged you, just like God has forgiven you in Christ. That's the basic definition of being a Christian. This doesn't have to get complicated. You don't need to call the person or have an intervention every single time. Simply drop to your knees right now and tell the Lord that you're letting that person go.

I'm sure there are situations that will require meetings and confessions and restitution, but for the majority of you, all it will take is the simple willingness to let the other person go, even when you feel wronged, even when you've been lied to, even when you deserve justice. Don't delay the obvious. Forgive freely as Christ has forgiven you, and trust God to work out the justice part.

3. Let Go of Your Past

There's a cheesy saying that goes like this: "The past is history, the future is a mystery, this moment is a gift, that's why we call it the present."[24] There is so much truth in that statement. Look, past mistakes often lead to negative consequences today, but no matter how hard you try, you cannot go back and change the past. In order for you to overcome the bitterness in your life, you must let go of your past. The more you review the past, with its sin and mistakes, the longer you'll be held in the clutches of bitterness. You are not living out plan B for your life. God isn't miffed at the way things turned out. Your life would not be better if _____. Those are all lies that you've believed, and it's time you let go of your past. God's sovereignty trumps your past, and He never makes mistakes.

Paul had a horrid past. He had killed so many Christians, including Stephen, the innocent martyr. He had cursed our Savior. Is it any wonder that God chose him to remind us that our past is behind us when he said in Philippians 3:13, "Forgetting what lies behind and straining forward to what lies ahead"?

God will use your past for His glory. Leave it to Him to do so when and how He chooses. As for you, turn your eyes upward to His face and thrive.

4. Let Go of Your Dreams

We all have them: dreams. We live for them. We chase them. And we're devastated when they don't come to pass. Sometimes we even idolize them. When that happens and our dreams fail, bitterness wraps itself around our hearts.

It may be time for you to give up your well-planned dreams and embrace the ones God has for you. I never dreamed my life would turn out like it did. The year after my second broken engagement, I changed jobs for a better one, I moved into a new house, I started a blog that continues to be read by hundreds today, and I took a job as the women's ministry director at my church. Talk about surprises!

Did I deserve any of these blessings? Many of you who are still hung up on the fact that I broke into my ex-fiancé's email would say no. But I'm blessed to have a merciful Father for my judge and get to live a life that is above and beyond what I could have ever imagined.

YOU ARE NOT living out plan B for your life.

Could I have done any of it without the broken heart and the lessons in forgiveness? Could I have done any of it with bitterness still clutched around my heart? I think you know the answer.

There is no past too shameful for God to erase; there is no sin too horrific for Him to forgive; and there is no bitterness too strong for Him to uproot.

He's a God I'm proud to call Father. He's a God I'm privileged to serve. I hope He's your Father too.

9

Joy Stealer:
Destroying Idolatry

Let's jump right into the third obstacle to overcome on the road to thriving: idolatry.

The first thing that may come to your mind when you think about an idol may be the little statue at your local Chinese restaurant, but the truth about idols is much more insidious. Idols have a way of creeping into every single Christian's life, robbing you of joy and true satisfaction.

This may come as a surprise to you, but the Bible has a lot to say about idols. The reason is that most of us struggle with idol worship. Instead of loving God with all of our hearts, we slowly turn to idols to satisfy us. Instead of turning to God to meet all of our needs, we find ourselves turning to things like food, porn, romance novels, exercise, or toxic relationships.

I should explain myself a little bit more by giving you a definition of an idol. An idol, biblically speaking, is any desire, ideal, or expectation that you worship, serve, and long for. All of a sudden, idolatry doesn't quite seem a thing of ancient history anymore, does it? Idols become much more personal and much more dangerous, luring our hearts away from the Lord Jesus Christ and closer and closer toward sin.

If you're still looking for the life that thrives, there is no room for idolatry in it. This is one obstacle you must overcome. Nothing will steal your joy like allowing your unmet desires to be filled with anything outside of the Lord Jesus Christ. If not guarded, your unmet desires will quickly become the road to idolatry in your life and will derail you from thriving.

While unmet desires are not restricted to singleness, they have a way of glaring in the life of the single Christian. Earlier in the book, we talked about how we were made to crave. God put a hunger in our soul to draw us closer to Himself. The minute we step out of His plan for our wholeness and embrace idols in our life to satisfy our needs, we come up empty and dissatisfied.

Consider your life right now. When you think about your unmet needs, are you turning to your idol to meet your need, or are you running to the Lord instead?

WE CAN BE deceived into thinking that a good thing cannot become an idol, but we ought to know better.

Let me take you back to the Corinthian Christians for a moment since we haven't picked on them for a while. Remember that the church in Corinth was a bit of a mess. One man was committing sexual immorality with his stepmother. The church was being heavily influenced by the culture. Sexual immorality was prevalent. Idol worship was the norm. The church wrote Paul, asking for help to navigate the messy waters. Paul jumped at the opportunity and wrote 1 Corinthians with some stern instructions about what it means to live in Christ and walk in Him. By the time he got to 1 Corinthians 7, he'd already established the sinfulness of sexual immorality and presented God's approach to love, sex, marriage, and singleness. But then suddenly, Paul switched gears in 1 Corinthians 8 to talk about foods and idols. Whoa, Nelly.

Idolatry was common back in those days. People worshiped idols and offered foods to idols as an act of worship. Some people also kept idols in their homes and relied on them for safety and blessing. The practice was sinful, and Paul needed to remind the Corinthian Christians of some basics on idol worship.

By the time Paul got to chapter 10, he pointed the Corinthian church all the way back to Moses and the people of Israel and used them as an example of the sinfulness of idolatry and its disastrous effect. In describing what happened to the people of Israel in the wilderness, Paul made a short leap, connecting idolatry to sexual immorality in verses 7–8: "Do not be idolaters as some of them were; as it is written, 'The people sat down to eat and drink and rose up to play.' We must not indulge in sexual immorality as some of them did, and twenty-three thousand fell in a single day."

Are you keeping up with this?

Paul took the Corinthian Christians all the way back to Exodus 32. Moses was up on the mountain getting the Ten Commandments. The people of Israel got tired of waiting for him, so they made an idol—a golden calf—and started worshiping it. As part of their worship, they indulged in sexual immorality. That day, God was so angered at the people of Israel that 23,000 people died. Were it not for Moses interceding, things may have been even worse. I'd say idol worship is a pretty serious offense, wouldn't you?

You're probably wondering what all that has to do with your life today. I'm glad you asked. Idol worship is not merely a thing of the past. Idol worship is a threat to every single Christian today. While we may not be making gold calves, we have our own version of idols—things we turn to for satisfaction instead of turning to the Lord.

I came up with a list of modern-day idols that Christians worship today. Check it out: pornography, video games, romance novels, same-sex relationships, toxic relationships (relationships that you know are bad for you but you hang on to anyway), food, exercise, television, the Internet, unnecessary spending on yet more material possessions for comfort, old boyfriends, masturbation, alcohol, cigarettes, pot, any illicit drug, and sometimes even your ministry activity.

If I missed your idol of your choice, simply add it to the list. We have too many idols to keep track of. Did the last one surprise you? We can be deceived into thinking that a good thing cannot become an idol, but we ought to know better. Christians sometimes use ministry activities for comfort to numb their conscience instead of turning to the Lord for true satisfaction. Busyness is far easier to revert to than intimacy with God. Your choices in life will reveal the true nature of your heart.

I've tried to be as honest as possible with you in this book, so why stop now? I've struggled with two idols in my life that nearly killed my relationship with the Lord. Let me tell you about them.

The first idol that slipped into my life is the idol of sex. I don't mean sex in the crass kind of way but great sex within the context of a married, God-honoring relationship. The more books I read, and the more movies I saw, the more convinced I was that everyone eventually found the big love, the soul mate, the perfect partner, then got married and had great sex (and all the married people laughed).

I DEVELOPED some unhealthy fantasies, fantasies that in today's world would be applauded and commended, but ones that I knew were sinful.

I couldn't understand why God would hold back something so good from me. In my twenties, I assumed He was just waiting to make it really, really good for me. In my thirties, I started having my doubts. What got me the most was the idea that there might not be sex in heaven. Being single didn't bother me too much. In fact, it would have been perfect for me had God created some outlet for my sexual desires. But that I would possibly miss out on something that seemed so good and not be able to ever experience it, even in heaven, just seemed hateful to me.

It didn't help that I have a vivid imagination and have been a voracious reader since my childhood. I remember reading literature as a twelve-year-old that was far too sophisticated for my immature mind—books by Hemingway, Maugham, and Fitzgerald—enough to get a teenager's hormonal imagination going. I developed some unhealthy fantasies, fantasies that in today's world would be applauded and commended, but ones that I knew were sinful.

What is interesting is that in my twenties, guilt was a good motivator to avoid the sins of the flesh. I didn't want my imagination to ruin the marital bed, as so many writers and preachers had warned me about, so I held off and did really well. I had years of victory over my sin. I knew that someday, God would honor my strength of character and provide the perfect man for me to enjoy the rest of my life with.

Then came my thirties. The first few years were uneventful, but after I ended the second engagement, I realized that I may never marry in this life, and that if and when I did, I'd be over my peak with a nonexistent sexual drive. That didn't seem fair.

I decided I'd had enough, and I gave up the battle. If God didn't make provision for me as a single Christian, I'd take matters into my own hands. Don't worry, I kept things Christian and respectable, but I had convinced myself that without an orgasm, I could not be happy. I chose my idol to bring me satisfaction but came up empty again and again.

I read this by C. S. Lewis once.

"I think our present outlook might be like that of a small boy who, on being told that the sexual act was the highest bodily pleasure should immediately ask whether you ate chocolates at the same time. On receiving the answer, No, he might regard absence of chocolates as the chief characteristic of sexuality. In vain would you tell him that the reason why lovers in their carnal raptures don't bother about chocolates is that they have something better to think of. The boy knows chocolate: he does not know the positive thing that excludes it. We are in the same position. We know the sexual life; we do not know, except in glimpses, the other thing which, in Heaven, will leave no room for it."[25]

Satan is an expert at fooling us into thinking that God is keeping something really good from us. He did it back in Genesis with Eve, and he'd done it with me. God isn't holding out on us. He isn't hateful or unfeeling. It's just that He sees the bigger picture. We, on the other hand, have to make the daily choice of where we will find our satisfaction. What I discovered through my idolatry is what Eve had found back in Genesis 3: instead of satisfying us, the fruit we desperately crave and go after only brings us shame. Sex had become an idol for me, and there was only one way out of it: total destruction of the idol.

I told you I've had two idols in my life, so it's only fair I mention the second: the idol of my looks. Generally speaking, on a scale of one to ten, I'd say I'm a six. When I clean up, I may even be a seven. I try to take good care of myself. I grew up in Lebanon where people really care about the way they look, and I am predisposed at baseline to mind the outside. But something dreadful happened to me in my late twenties: I got plagued with adult acne.

I CONVINCED myself that I could have endured persecution better than this struggle with my skin.

To borrow from Dickens: "It was the best of times; it was the worst of times."[26] No, really it was the worst of times. I can count the zits I had as a teenager on one hand, so to say that I wasn't prepared for this struggle is an understatement. I saw more doctors and tried more remedies than I can tell you. But this battle wasn't about my skin; it was about my heart. I quickly went from simply wanting to look good to becoming obsessed with my face, idolizing a clear complexion above all else. I knew that God could heal me, so why wasn't He doing it? If God were good, He'd fix my little problem. Wouldn't He? It made no sense to me. I was convinced that I'd be perfectly happy if God would just heal me. This was an even bigger deal for me than the sex because it was so visual and obvious for everyone to see. I couldn't hide it. How could God allow me, a sold-out Christian, to suffer this way?

It sounds so petty to tell you about it now, but Satan is so good at making little things seem so big. I remember walking into the ER one day when I was feeling particularly low, and a five-year-old girl pointed to something on my face and innocently asked, "What's that on your face?" Another time, a mother recommended I use my first morning urine on my face as a home remedy. Don't worry—I did not follow her advice, but I'm still amazed at how strategic Satan is about bringing God's children down. Things got pretty low for me during that season of my life.

I convinced myself that I could have endured persecution better than this struggle with my skin. Much to my shame, my outlook on life got so bad that I quit leading my small group at one point because I was so frustrated with the Lord for not fixing my problem when He could have so easily done so.

But God had other plans for me. His plan was to use the very thing that I hated the most to teach me. I started noticing that when my skin was clear, I felt loved by God, and when it wasn't, I felt unloved by God. My appearance had become my idol. God was in the process of destroying the idol and my pride along with it.

I share my struggles with you in horrific detail to show you that idolatry isn't something someone else struggles with. It's far closer to home than we'd like it to be. In case you missed the context, my struggle with idolatry took place shortly after I had accepted God's call for my life for ministry. I was reading and studying my Bible daily and teaching Bible studies, while my heart was torn on these two issues. On the outside, I was a model Christian. Frankly, even in these struggles, I wasn't trying to be rebellious, but I still had so much to learn about God and His love toward me. I still had to learn that God alone was sufficient to meet all of my needs. I was still to understand His goodness to me. I was still to grasp the understanding that He is God and I am not.

By God's grace, I continue to learn. I've found that God is far more patient with us than we deserve. He is longsuffering but will not stop with us until we give Him our full surrender and complete obedience. Today He has mine, and I've never been happier.

If you're still wondering whether you have an idol in your life, let me give you four ways to help you diagnose yourself.

DIAGNOSING IDOLATRY IN YOUR HEART

Idols have a way of creeping up on you when you least expect it. Think about your life and your desires. Consider these four statements and see if any of them describe you:

Without it, I won't be happy.

Think about your life. Think about what you think you need to be happy. It doesn't have to be big. It could be your mortgage, or the involvement of your ex-husband in the life of your child. Whatever you think you need to make you happy will threaten to become an idol in your life. If you believe marriage is the only thing that will make you happy, bingo! You've found your idol. Satan's greatest lie is that you need something outside of the Lord Jesus Christ to give you happiness. Don't believe it.

Without it, I doubt God's love for me.

If you're convinced that God doesn't love you because He hasn't done _____, then that thing has become your idol. For me, for a while, it was a clear complexion. For you it may be a friendship, a material possession, a place. You figure it out.

The truth is that God loves you so much that He died for you while you were still a sinner. And He loves you just as much today. It may be time for you to get rid of the notion of an impersonal God who doesn't care about your deepest needs, and embrace the God of the Bible who loves you unconditionally. He loves you even if you'll never get the one thing you think you can't live without, because He knows the truth: He's the one thing—the only thing—you can't live without. By the way—that thing you're hinging God's love on—that's your idol.

WHATEVER YOU think you need to make you happy will threaten to become an idol in your life.

"Without it" is not an option.

If you want something so bad that you'll go to any extreme to get it, no matter who gets hurt in the process, and no matter the consequences, you may be dealing with an idol. That's how the Israelites acted in Exodus 32. While Moses was up on the mountain with God, the people got sick of waiting. Waiting was no longer an option for them. So they took matters into their hands. They made an idol, and *voila!* They found any warm body, became sexually immoral, and that day 23,000 people died.

Watch out if you're tempted to quit waiting on the Lord and want to take matters into your own hands. Some of you have tried that route and found yourselves still living out the consequences of that choice. It's never a good idea to give God ultimatums. He's the God of the universe. I wouldn't go there if I were you. And that thing you think you can't live without, that's your idol.

Without it, my life is not worth living.

Your desires left unchecked could bring you to a place where you feel like your life is not worth living without the thing you desire. That's a sad place to be. I hope I'm not describing you, and I hope you don't stay in this place for long. God loves you. He gave you your desires with one goal in mind: to turn you toward Him through your desires. You were made to worship Him. I hope you turn your eyes to Him and find freedom along with the life that thrives.

You should have a pretty good idea by now of whether you're dealing with an idol in your life. I've already told you about my struggle with idolatry in my life. I never set out to worship an idol, but as self-pity took over, and as bitterness dug its roots deeper, my trust in God's goodness wavered. I found myself refusing to turn to the Lord to meet my needs, something I would have thought unthinkable earlier in my life. I started believing the lie that God could not meet my needs. I convinced myself that all that God had given me was not quite enough so long as He didn't provide me with my "happily ever after," or my Proactiv face. I became obsessed with the one thing I wanted but didn't have, and pretty soon I found myself dancing around my self-made golden calf—until God in His mercy stopped me and won my heart back.

In Isaiah 44:20, God describes the idol worshiper like this: "He feeds on ashes; a deluded heart has led him astray." By God's grace, my season of feeding on ashes did not last long. By God's grace, He is the only One I worship today. Learn from the Israelites. Learn from the Corinthian church, and learn from me.

God hates idolatry, and it must be destroyed. Let's find out how.

DESTROYING THE IDOLS IN YOUR HEART

The antidote to worshiping any man-made idol is the worship of the One you were created for—the Lord Jesus Christ. If the thing you desire has become more important to you than God, then you've got an idol on your hands, and it's time to take some pretty drastic measures.

1. It Will Involve a Battle

In Exodus 32, after Moses came down from the mountain and saw the people worshiping the golden calf, he freaked out. Well, that's not the biblical term, but he was really very upset. Moses then did what every person must do in the face of an idol. He got out his sword and got ready to fight. Check it out for yourself in Exodus 32:27.

WHEN I STRUGGLE against temptation and don't find easy victory, I scratch my head and wonder where I went wrong.

Getting rid of the idol in your life is not going to be easy. It will entail a battle. I like the terminology in Hebrews 12:4 as it pertains to our struggle with sin. The writer says, "In your struggle against sin you have not yet resisted to the point of shedding your blood."

For the most part, I find myself to be a comfort-seeking creature. I want holiness, but I want it easily. I want purity, but I don't want to work really hard for it. When I struggle against temptation and don't find easy victory, I scratch my head and wonder where I went wrong. If this sounds familiar to you, it's because we are not living with a warlike mentality. We resent struggling to the point of shedding of blood. Fighting off your idols is not easy work, but it's necessary work and it's God-honoring work.

Unlike Moses, our battles won't involve real swords. Our battles will involve the sword of the Spirit—the Word of God (Ephesians 6:17). In order to win the battle against idolatry, you will need to fight it first in your mind and then with your will.

The turning point for me, in my battle against idolatry, didn't come with some whimsical feeling or divine apparition. God's way is much simpler, and yet much harder. His Word is the truth. We must accept it regardless of our feelings, or we can choose to reject it and die. At the height of my dissatisfaction and weakening intimacy with the Lord, I had to agree with God's Word or remain in my mess. I was worshiping an idol and looking to it for joy, but I was miserable. I took a step of faith and the Lord helped me fight the battle in full force in my mind. I fought it the only way God has given us: with His Word. Second Corinthians 10:3–5 says this: "For though we walk in the flesh, we are not waging war according to the flesh. For the weapons of our warfare are not of the flesh but have divine power to destroy strongholds. We destroy arguments and every lofty opinion raised against the knowledge of God, and take every thought captive to obey Christ."

At my church, we like to say that "faith is believing God's

Word and acting on it no matter how you feel, knowing that God promises a good result." It's not until you step into the Jordan that you will see the waters spread and the way open for you. If you're still waiting for your "Aha!" moment to start obeying the Lord, you'll be waiting a long time. Obedience is an act of faith. So get ready for battle, and soon you will see the victory!

2. It Will Demand Your Choice

Back in Exodus 32, when Moses came down from the mountain and saw his idol-worshiping brothers, he drew his sword and asked a key question: "Who is on the Lord's side? Come to me" (Exodus 32:26).

That day, the sons of Levi gathered around Moses, and they killed 3,000 of their own brothers. That seems drastic to our Western, politically correct minds. But God was pleased with the sons of Levi, and He was pleased with Moses. In your fight against idolatry in your life, whose side will you choose? And how serious are you about holiness?

Each time you revert to your idol for comfort instead of turning to the Lord, you are choosing against the Lord. But each time you resist the temptation in your life, you are aligning yourself with Moses and the sons of Levi. Do you see it? It is a big deal, but the choice is yours.

EACH TIME you revert to your idol for comfort instead of turning to the Lord, you are choosing against the Lord.

3. It Will Cost You Something

On the day that Moses fought the idol worshipers, 3,000 men died, and later on God sent a plague that killed another 20,000 men. That seems like a high price to pay for worshiping an idol, but God would have it no other way. Don't doubt for a second that in fighting off the idols in your life, you will have a price to pay. The price of disobedience is high. It will cost you something every single time.

For some of you, killing your idol may mean the death of a relationship you treasure so much. For others, it may mean throwing out your TV or your computer or your smartphone. I had to get rid of my Kindle app, then my iPad. It may be even more drastic for you. You may have to move out of your home or your town or change jobs.

The question you need to answer is this: How far are you willing to go to destroy the idol in your life? If you're not willing to go all the way, you may not be ready to destroy that idol yet.

If you're wondering why God demands such a high price, let me remind you of the price He paid for you. He gave His life. That's how costly your salvation was. Does that change things a bit for you? Salvation was not cheap, how dare we live a cheap grace and cling to our sins and our idols when Jesus gave His all for us?

4. God Always Makes a Way Out

The thing I love the most about God is that He doesn't leave us hanging. He knows how difficult the task of destroying idols is. He understands how luring sexual immorality is. So He throws in 1 Corinthians 10:12–13, a verse for the ages: "Therefore let anyone who thinks that he stands take heed lest he fall. No temptation has overtaken you that is not common to man. God is faithful, and he will not let you be tempted beyond your ability, but with the temptation he will also provide the way of escape, that you may be able to endure it."

This is incredible. First of all, God reminds us that none of us are immune. So there's no reason for you to feel haughty. We're on the same level playing field. If you've been reading this chapter and thinking to yourself that you're okay when it comes to idolatry, think again. It could happen to you too!

But even better is the news that God has given us a way out. In His faithfulness, He knows a better way. This better way is given in verse 14: "Flee from idolatry." Flee means that you must drop everything and run—fast! God's way for us to escape our idols is to run! Check yourself: How fast are you running? Do you need a new pair of running shoes?

God is faithful. Do you know that Exodus 32 was not the last time the Israelites chose to worship an idol instead of worshiping God? Over the course of their history, Israel fell into idol worship over and over again. But God in His faithfulness still calls them His children. He remains faithful to His own, even to this day. That's who He is.

One more thing I should mention—in Exodus 32, the people needed an intercessor to receive God's forgiveness, and Moses became that person. In post-resurrection Christianity, Christ is the only intercessor we need. We can ask for forgiveness directly from God because Christ has already paid the price for our sin and is sitting on the right hand of God, making intercession for us.

Indeed Christ does make a way for us in more ways than one. He shed His blood for our redemption. He meets our need through His sufficiency. And He makes a way of escape through His faithfulness.

He is so worthy of our worship.

10

Never Alone:
Rejecting the Lie
of Loneliness

The last obstacle to overcome as you aim toward the life that thrives is an obstacle that every single Christian knows all too well. It's the obstacle of loneliness.

Let me be honest with you. I like living alone. I have lived alone since I turned twenty. I enjoy solitude and quietness. Call me crazy, but I'm one of those people who don't like the sound of television or even a radio in my house. It gets on my nerves. I like to be alone. Even as I'm writing this book, I'm way up north in Wisconsin where I lack WiFi and have poor cell phone reception. When I do get a little reception and call home, I'm asked if I'm going nuts being all alone or if I'm bored. The words sound foreign to me. I'm in heaven.

Yet once in a while, when I least expect it, I find myself pummeled by an avalanche of loneliness so overwhelming and so deep it knocks me over.

It usually happens late at night. I leave the ER at the end of a long shift. I have a forty-five-minute drive home, and it's never easy. I'm usually sleepy, struggling to keep my eyes open. I'm always thankful for the rumble strips on the edge of the highway. Some people talk about being too wound up to sleep after a shift in the ER. I've never had that problem. I'm always beat, ready for bed.

Once in a while, if I haven't managed my eating schedule well, I feel hungry. Hunger trumps sleep almost every time in my Western mindset. We resent going to bed hungry in America. Usually ice cream will do, but not too much of it. If you eat too much dairy after midnight, it has a way of sticking to the roof of your mouth the next morning. Alternatively, orange juice is a great staple at two in the morning. If you're single like me, you don't have to use a cup for OJ, which means you don't have to wash a cup either. It's a small but added bonus. They say it's the little things that count. I tend to agree.

It's eerily quiet at night, except in the summer when the crickets keep me company. Their sound is rhythmic. It soothes me, and for a while, I don't feel so lonely. It doesn't matter how busy my day has been, or how many people will surround me tomorrow. At night, the thought of people seems foreign, far.

I tell myself that tomorrow I'll miss being alone. I'll fondly think of these quiet hours of night interrupted only by cicadas' whispers, and the moon hung low in the sky. But in that moment, in the middle of the night, I'm alone in my house, I'm alone in my town, I'm alone in the world.

I have a fleeting thought about God. I grab on to it. I let it settle over me. And in the middle of the night I'm gently reminded . . .

I am near.

I am here.

I finally surrender and sleep.

If you're single, you know exactly that kind of loneliness I just described. You've felt it more often than you care to admit. You've battled the questions that come with loneliness, the sense of abandonment by God, by friends, by the church, and you're hoping for some answers.

It doesn't matter if you live in New York City or Jackson, Mississippi, loneliness is real and it can take epic proportions.

Loneliness is the deep aching pain that plagues every single Christian at some point or another. It's the isolation that comes from living in an increasingly independent society where everyone prefers the pleasure of their own company to yours.

I'm not talking about solitude. Solitude is welcome to most busy people. Solitude is finding yourself resting in a quiet and finally empty house on a Saturday evening after a busy week of guests and people. Your time has been stretched, your patience worn, and you relish the quiet solitude of the hour and are grateful for its soothing peace.

TODAY, INDEPENDENCE finds many adults suffering from isolation and aloneness so deep that little can soothe the hurt that stems from its wound.

Loneliness is different. It's lonely and it's quiet. It's still. It's one in a world of twos.

It didn't always used to be this way. In fact, it's not this way in many other places outside of the United States. I grew up in Lebanon where community is still a huge part of life. Too huge, one could argue. If you sneeze, your aunt Soumayya calls to ask if you're coming down with a cold. If you spill the coffee, there's a chance you'll make the evening news. It's considered a sign of love and commitment to one another to know everything there is to know about your life. It's a sign of caring.

Somewhere in the spectrum of civilization and westernization came the notion that people wanted more independence. Financial success welcomed the idea of moving out of your parents' home and finding a place of your own. Yet today, independence finds many adults suffering from isolation and aloneness so deep that little can soothe the hurt that stems from its wound.

So people get married, thinking that another human being will obliterate their loneliness. It helps a little at first. But one day, out of the random blue, that loneliness that was meant to be kept at bay lifts its ugly head and plops itself in the middle of your home, reminding you of the fact that even your husband cannot totally satisfy you and that your wife does not really understand you like you need her to.

Meanwhile, single people everywhere dream of marriage as their answer to loneliness.

If you've ever struggled with loneliness, you're not alone. Most single Christians have struggled with it at some point or another. Few are the singles who find a community like in the show *Friends* and spend their evenings with beautiful people over lattes in a hip coffee shop in New York City. (If that's you, good for you. The rest of us are drinking our same old Starbucks, alone, in Anytown, USA.)

I'd like to uncover some of the reasons that single Christians struggle with loneliness.

REASONS FOR LONELINESS

Loneliness of Sin

I can't talk about the reasons for loneliness and not mention the most obvious and least considered one. If you're a child of God and are living a lifestyle of willful disobedience to God, you have likely found yourself in the trenches of loneliness. Isaiah 59:2 says it this way: "But your iniquities have made a separation between you and your God, and your sins have hidden his face from you so that he does not hear."

When you choose to sin, you choose to widen the gap of intimacy that your soul craves between you and the Lord. God doesn't disown you or throw you out of His family when you sin, but you will feel a growing separation from Him. If you pray and feel like your prayers simply hit the ceiling, it could be that you have unconfessed sin in your life. Ask the Lord to search your heart for it, and then hurry up and come clean.

Loneliness of Transition

You've just moved, you don't know anyone in your new town. You're too old and too tired to do anything about it. It's Friday night, and you think everyone else in the world is out having some fun while your life is slowly ticking away, one dragging minute at a time. That's the loneliness that comes from the transitions of life, and it's not uncommon for most single Christians to feel at some point or another.

You try spending an evening at church with other single people, but you find it hard to plug in. Most of them have known each other for years—which only exacerbates your sense of loneliness.

I spent the years between sixteen and thirty living in one place no longer than four years. I get the loneliness of transition, and it only gets harder the older I get!

Loneliness of Breaking Up

Breaking up is hard to do. You may not have seen it coming, even though possibly everyone else in your life did. You're bewildered by it, not sure how the relationship you thought was so good could end up so broken. You feel sorry for yourself. You feel the deep, aching loneliness that only a person who has felt the sting of rejection fully understands.

Trust me, having ended two engagements, I understand the loneliness of breaking up. I wrote some of my best poems right after my breakups. I bet I could have turned into a country western star had I tried. Nothing anyone says helps lessen this kind of loneliness. It's a loneliness that leaves you reeling and feeling like nothing will ever get better in your life. Don't believe them. It does get better.

Loneliness of Isolation

This is a self-induced loneliness that may stem from a number of reasons. You may have been hurt by some friends, or are going through a season of self-pity where you'd rather not talk to anyone. I've experienced this kind of loneliness, and it's not pretty. Proverbs 18:1 says it like this: "Whoever isolates himself seeks his own desire; he breaks out against all sound judgment."

The loneliness of isolation refuses the options for relationship that God has provided. I remember isolating myself extremely well during my struggle with acne. I didn't want to be seen. I felt insecure and afraid, so I locked myself up most of the time. I still made it to church, but tried hard not to look anyone in the eye, lest they venture to talk to me. I even avoided my own family during that time, out of the depth of my insecurities.

You may not struggle with acne, but you have your own issues that may be separating you from your church family. Watch out if you're isolating yourself that way. You're setting yourself up to sin and putting yourself in a spiritually vulnerable place.

Loneliness of Spiritual Opposition

Every Christian living in obedience to the Lord will sense this kind of loneliness. It's the loneliness of spiritual attack. It's the loneliness of spiritual oppression. It comes out of nowhere. It has no clear explanation. And it will demand every ounce of spiritual focus to fight it. The worst thing you can do when you feel the loneliness of opposition is to ignore God's Word and try to analyze the problem. Watch out for this kind of loneliness if you've just taken a step of faith in ministry, or in obedience to the Lord.

HIS PRESENCE is closer than you think.

The upside of this kind of loneliness is that you can turn it into a time of worshipful solitude and use it to seek Christ's face more dearly. Jesus set the example often of separating Himself from His group of disciples in order to seek uninterrupted communion with His Father. If Jesus needed this time alone with God the Father, don't you think you need it too?

Loneliness has many causes. It comes in a variety of styles and colors. And it must be overcome in order to thrive. The best place to begin overcoming this obstacle is to look at what God says about loneliness. Does God's Word have any ideas for you for overcoming loneliness? Are there steps to take to overcome loneliness? Let's find out.

HOW TO OVERCOME LONELINESS

If you want to know what I do as an ER doctor, I can sum it up to two things: I find out what the problem is, and I fix it.

At this point, I hope you've diagnosed the reason for your loneliness. Now let's get a plan to fix it.

Recognize the Truth of God's Presence

The first step in overcoming loneliness is to recognize the lie of loneliness. The truth is that you are never alone. When you accepted Christ as your Savior, He came to live in you. You are never alone. Christ is always with you. His presence is closer than you think.

You don't have to feel His presence to know He is near.

You simply have to take His word for it. Proclaim God's presence by faith. In Hebrews 13:5 God promises this: "I will never leave you nor forsake you." He will not leave you when you sin. He will not leave you when you forget about Him. He will not leave you when you have indigestion. He is with you all the time.

In fact, God wants to use your loneliness to draw your attention to Him. Instead of hiding in your shell of self-pity, the next time you feel lonely, try looking to the Lord instead of turning the television on.

David did that. He often felt lonely. I love these verses that David wrote in the Psalms: "I am like a desert owl of the wilderness, like an owl of the waste places; I lie awake; I am like a lonely sparrow on the housetop" (Psalm 102:6–7).

David was a bit melodramatic, but I love the imagery he uses and confess that I connect with it more than I care to admit. Of course he spends twenty-eight verses in that chapter reviewing who God is and asking for His help. If you know anything about the life of David, you know that God answered him every single time!

Grow Your God-Given Relationships

I've always struggled with Genesis 2. After God created Adam, He said, "It is not good that the man should be alone" (Genesis 2:18). Yet many single Christians will often complain that God has allowed them to be alone. It's easy to get confused and resentful. If God thinks it's a bad idea for me to be alone, why has He withheld a husband?

The answer is not as complicated as we like to make it. God did in fact create human beings for relationship. The most important relationship He has created us for is a relationship with Him through His Son, Jesus Christ. God sent His son to die for us in order to secure our relationship to Him. He gave all that He is to ensure that we would never be alone.

The next time you complain that God has not given you any relationships to enjoy, remember Jesus Christ and look to Him for joy.

God has not only given us an unbreakable relationship with Himself, but He has also given us the body of Christ, His church, for relationship. If you're not part of a Bible-believing church, you're missing it. God's program for relationship is first through Himself, and then through His church.

I know, I know. Most single Christians are yelling throughout the book that no one in your church loves you, and that no one in your church understands you or has ever reached out to you, and that you often feel marginalized and isolated at church. Hang in there.

I believe that may be true half of the time. The church, after all, is not perfect. It is made up of sinners just like you and me, concerned primarily about their own lives and their own difficult circumstances much like you and I are too.

YOU'RE GOING to have to stop waiting for others in the church to reach out to you, and take that first step of faith yourself.

No matter how wonderful your church is, you may still find yourself alone, misunderstood, and sad. Sooner or later, you're going to have to stop waiting for others in the church to reach out to you and take that first step of faith yourself.

I had to do that once. It occurred to me one day that instead of waiting for others to minister to me, I should start ministering to them. I had been a follower of Christ for some time by that point and had no excuse for simply sitting back and watching. So I did. Before I knew it, I had more friends than I knew what to do with and was asked to teach a women's Bible study. The next thing I knew, God had called me into full-time ministry.

That was thirteen years ago and the rest, as they say, is history. Since those days, I have had my share of lonely days, but instead of blaming the church for it, I've tried to love it instead. As a growing follower of Jesus Christ, I finally understand that the church needs me just as much as I need the church. Will you love it for His sake? You may be surprised and find in it a well of relationships when you do.

Reorder Your Pain

Most people make a whole lot more about their personal pain than they need to. I see it often in my practice in the ER. I'll walk in a room and see a kid sitting on the bed calmly watching TV, smiling, with a normal heart rate, and a normal blood pressure. I'll ask how bad his pain is, and he'll suddenly scrunch up his nose and tell me his pain is a ten out of ten. This kid clearly has a wrong view of his pain. It's not that the kid doesn't have pain—otherwise he wouldn't be in the ER—but his pain doesn't quite seem as bad as he's convinced

211

himself and his mother that it is.

You may be in the same boat when it comes to the pain of your singleness. Sure, you may have true pain; there's no reason to deny it. But perhaps the pain of your loneliness ought to be placed back in its proper order again.

Single Christians can get so caught up in self-pity and the ache of loneliness that an evening alone can turn into a personal crisis and the certainty that God has abandoned them. I speak from personal experience. As you grow in your relationship with the Lord, you must learn not to exaggerate the pain of your loneliness and make an effort to stop rehearsing it over and over again. The less you dwell on your loneliness, the less you will see it as a bitter pill to swallow, and the more you will embrace it as a pathway to the very heart of God.

Guard against It

I mentioned the reasons for loneliness earlier to help you recognize your triggers for it and guard against them. You will need to be strategic in your planning. Think about the things that cause you to feel lonely. If constantly measuring your life against others brings on a sense of loneliness, get rid of your Facebook account. If watching romantic comedies on TBS makes you feel lonely, cancel your cable subscription and stop renting movies. If not getting regular eHarmony dates makes you lonely, cancel eHarmony. If Friday nights are your bad nights, make plans ahead of time to be with friends on Friday nights. And if you have adult onset acne and can't face looking at another human being, come over to my house. I'll commiserate with you, and then I'll gently remind you of what God says in His Word in 1 Samuel 16:7. It's what my eight-year-old nephew still tells me on my off days. "Do not look on his appearance or on the height of his stature, because I have rejected him. For the Lord sees not as man sees: man looks on the outward appearance, but the Lord looks on the heart."

That's great, isn't it?

The sooner you get rid of the things that welcome your loneliness, the better off you'll be. It's the only way you'll thrive.

Renew Your Mind

I get lonely when I get in a "me-centered" mentality. The best way I've found to overcome such self-centered thoughts is by washing my mind with the Word of God and renewing my thoughts with His truth. I've found a few key verses that are a great reminder for me when I feel as if God is far away.

Remember that we're in a battle. The fight is not always easy, but victory is secure. The strategy of constantly renewing your mind means that you can't just rely on your morning quiet time to carry you through if you're mostly struggling at night. You may have to actually read your Bible twice that day. Imagine that!

LONELINESS can become a comfortable companion for the single Christian.

It is in the midst of your struggle that you must get out the sword of God's Word and fight the battle that is raging in your mind. I have found that steady memorization of God's Word is also helpful in overcoming my loneliness. God is faithful to bring His Word to mind in my time of need. Your transformation from shriveling Christian to thriving Christian happens as you renew your mind, one battle at a time.

Turn Your Focus on to Others

Loneliness can become a comfortable companion for the single Christian, but in order to thrive, you have to get out of your comfort zone and reach out to other people. I don't mean to sound like a Christian infomercial, but the truth is that when you do, you will meet many people—both single and married—who are going through much greater suffering than you are. There are so many ways to help others in our society of hurting people. Try volunteering at the soup kitchen, or start a ministry to the widows in your church. Help out with children's ministry at your church—they always need more helpers. Life is short. The harvest is plentiful. Get working for God! It's the surest way to take your attention off of yourself and your lonely plight, and focus it on others.

I have always loved Corrie ten Boom. Here was a woman who understood how to overcome loneliness in the midst of her singleness. Though you may know Corrie ten Boom as a war hero, you may be surprised to find out that as a young woman, Corrie fell in love with a man who would end the relationship she thought was headed toward marriage and marry another woman instead. Her father said something very wise. "Corrie, do you know what hurts so very much?

It's love. Love is the strongest force in the world, and when it is blocked that means pain. There are two things we can do when this happens: We can kill the love so that it stops hurting. But then of course part of us dies, too. Or, Corrie, we can ask God to open up another route for that love to travel."[27]

History has revealed the choice Corrie made and countless lives will spend eternity thanking her for choosing love in the midst of her loneliness.

Loneliness can be a wilderness. But it can also be a pathway to God. Which will it be for you?

PART 4

Making It Happen

11

All You Need Is Love: Finding True Love in Christ

I remember my first crush. I was in the seventh grade, wore braces, had a bad perm, and talked way too fast. He was tall, blond, and perfect—a regular Adonis. His eyes were a deep sea blue and his smile a mile wide. And he had absolutely no idea who I was. That didn't change the fact that I wanted to marry him and bear his children, or that my heart beat out of my chest every time I eyed him on the other side of the playground.

I was in love, and baby, I knew that it was only a matter of time before the object of my love would wake up and figure out that I was the perfect girl for him.

He never did. A few months later, he and his family packed everything up and moved from Beirut to the United States of America and I never heard of him again. My heart was broken. Life would never be the same. I recently even tried finding him on Facebook but found no vestige of him, thus making him forever the one who never would be.

IF LOVE IS all a person needs, then the single Christian has a big problem.

Whether you're in the seventh grade (I hope you're not reading this book if you're in seventh grade), or just turned seventy, you know exactly what I'm talking about. You and I were made for love. We want love. We seek love. And we're disappointed when we don't fall in love. The Beatles crooned their lyrics, "Love is all you need," mesmerizing a lost world desperately in search for love and convincing us that the answer to all of our problems in life is to fall in love.

If love is all a person needs, then the single Christian has a big problem.

Why would God create you to love and not provide an object for your love?

What kind of God would place in you a longing for oneness with another being, and then leave you hanging?

The tension that single Christians face is palpable. The questions loom, becoming whispered prayers, but they are rarely spoken out loud.

Can the single Christian thrive without love? It is a question that demands an answer. If love is necessary for your soul to thrive, then where in the world do you find love? Surely God's perfect plan for the single Christian extends beyond a life of unrequited love and unfulfilled longings reminiscent of my seventh-grade heartbreak!

If you're still reading this book, I'm going to venture to

guess that you're really interested in the life that thrives. So far I've given you five attitudes to embrace in order to thrive, and I've covered four obstacles that you must overcome to thrive.

But I've left out a missing link—the secret sauce, so to speak. It's time to uncover the secret to the life that thrives. It's time to talk about what makes thriving possible. It's time to give you the key to executing the life that thrives.

I'll quit with the drama and simply lay it out for you clearly: love is the missing link that makes it all happen. Love is the Holy Grail, the magic bullet, the oil that makes the engine run. And this love is freely available to every single Christian who will accept it through the Lord Jesus Christ.

God's plan for your life is not a series of dos and don'ts intended to defeat you. God's plan for you is not to robotically and systematically become a better version of yourself by trying really hard to put on the right attitudes and getting rid of the wrong ones, though that may be part of the process. God's plan is better. His plan works because it begins and ends with love. He made you to love. He made you *for* love. He made you in order to demonstrate His love for you. And He's done it through His Son, Jesus Christ.

Here's how He explains it in Romans 5:8: "God shows his love for us in that while we were still sinners, Christ died for us."

That kind of love is pretty incredible. You can have all the head knowledge in the world and still shrivel up without love. Don't you think it's time we move beyond head knowledge and tackle the heart part?

I'd say it's time for every single Christian to reclaim true love.

FINDING TRUE LOVE IN CHRIST

You can't love someone you don't know. I thought I loved my seventh-grade crush, but all I had was the dreamy-eyed fantasy of a thirteen-year-old hormonal nerd. My mind took on a life of its own but had no basis in reality and led to great disappointment and utter failure.

Christ's love is different. It is real. It is lasting. It is abundant life. And it is everything you're looking for in your life and more.

God's desire for every single Christian is a thriving relationship with Him through the perfect love of Jesus Christ. It is only as you understand Christ's love for you and start drawing from it that you will truly thrive. The best way to understand Christ's love for you is by getting to know Him and by understanding His unchanging character.

YOUR PROBLEM is not that you don't know the Lord Jesus Christ and His love, but that you've forgotten all about it.

The story of Christ's love for you is a simple story that you may or may not have heard before. God loved you so much that He sent His only Son, Jesus Christ, to be born of a virgin named Mary. He lived perfectly for thirty-three years until He was unjustly crucified on a cross. It was horrible, but it was the whole reason for His coming to earth in the first place. God knew that man was separated from God because of sin and needed a Savior. So He sent His Son to earth as God incarnate with one purpose in mind: to die on a tree for your sin and mine. As unjust as His crucifixion was, it was done for you. It was done to give you eternal and abundant life. And it was done because of love. It was Christ's death on the cross that purchased your forgiveness.

If you're looking for true love, you don't need to look any further. Whether you've heard the facts before or if this is the first time you hear them, now is the time you receive them. Why don't you stop reading right now and pray this prayer:

Father, I know I'm a sinner and desperately need a Savior. I believe that You sent Your Son to die for my sin. I believe that Christ lived a perfect life and died without cause, simply to take away my sin. I receive this free gift You've given me and accept Your gift of love. From here on out, I want to trust You as my Savior and Lord, and I give You my life. In Jesus' name I pray, Amen.

If you just prayed this prayer, then you've turned a whole new page in your life. You just took your first step toward thriving. In fact, you may want to go back and read this book all over again. It will make a lot more sense to you now.

Most of you who picked up this book have already accepted Christ's love into your hearts. But somewhere between accepting Christ's love and waking up single, your love for Christ has waned and your trust in Him has wavered. You're disillusioned by God, and you're not sure why you pray since God never seems to answer. Christ on the cross was perfect for your salvation but seems to have little effect on your day-to-day life.

Your problem is not that you don't know the Lord Jesus Christ and His love, but that you've forgotten all about it. You need a basic reminder of who Christ is. I'm not suggesting a superficial knowledge. Think back to my seventh-grade crush. I could pick out the love of my life in a crowd, but I had no idea who he really was. In order to really know someone, you've got to get to know that person's character. A person's character describes the essence of that person.

Your love for Christ will grow as you understand God's character and hang on to it with all of your might, especially in your time of need. God's character will be your anchor as you seek the life that thrives. I'd like to give you four aspects of God's character that will help you thrive.

TRUSTING GOD'S CHARACTER
IS NECESSARY FOR THRIVING

The apostle Paul is an amazing example of a thriving single Christian. But he didn't start out that way. Earlier in his life, Paul was this guy who thought he was living well. He was highly educated and greatly respected. He was religious and rich. He was a force to be reckoned with by his peers, but he was far from thriving.

One day, as he was headed to Damascus to kill more Christians who trusted in Jesus Christ as their Savior and Messiah, Paul had a life-changing experience. A great light appeared to Paul, and he saw the risen Christ. Paul immediately recognized Christ as Lord. His first words to Christ were, "Who are you, Lord?" (Acts 9:5).

Paul's life was radically changed. He gave up his career, his friends, his family, his religion, and became the strongest and most respected leader in the early Christian church. By the time Paul wrote 1 Corinthians, he had been a follower of Jesus Christ for a few years and his love for Jesus Christ was still red-hot and blazing. His love remains contagious to us today.

What was Paul's secret for his transformation from chief of all sinners to chief of all saints? How did Paul radically embrace the life that thrives?

The answer has nothing to do with Paul and everything to do with Jesus Christ. From the moment Paul met the risen Christ, he had a clear vision and understanding of Christ's character that would set the tone for the rest of his life. No matter where Paul found himself—in prison, being beaten, or in the midst of a shipwreck in the worst storm of his life—Paul hung on to God's character with a fierceness that would do us good to emulate.

The result for Paul was a life that thrived. He thrived like no one else did. He flourished and blossomed and was fully satisfied, and this greatly magnified God. Margaret Clarkson has said this about singleness: "Why singleness? That the works of God might be made manifest in the deepest recesses of our beings. To declare God's glory in a fallen world. To show that God is enough for the human heart. To demonstrate to earth and hell the triumph of the life of God in the soul of man."[28]

Paul exemplified such a Christian life. Here was a man who understood that happiness and fullness of joy come not from marriage but from an understanding of who God is.

Here was a man who grasped the truth of God's character, allowing him to live a contented, self-controlled, and holy life of undivided devotion. Here was a man who refused to allow self-pity and bitterness to creep in, who shunned idols, and turned to Christ alone in his loneliness, making him the best model of a single Christian you could ever have.

HIS GOODNESS overflows into your life even when you don't recognize it.

I'd like to give you four aspects of God's character that Paul hung on to, allowing him to thrive in the most difficult circumstances:

1. God Is Good

Eve fell for it in the garden of Eden, so there's no reason to think that you won't too. Near-perfect Eve had everything: great looks, a great body, an amazing and hardworking husband who didn't hog the TV remote, and no in-laws. If anyone was set up to thrive, it was Eve. But there was one thing she couldn't have: the fruit. So naturally, the fruit became the one thing she couldn't get her mind and eyes off of. Day after day after day, she circled the tree and wondered about the forbidden fruit. But it's the way that she finally fell that should surprise us the most.

Satan knew exactly how to get Eve. All he had to do was convince her that God simply wasn't good. If God were good, He wouldn't hold anything back from Eve, would He? And poor Eve fell for it. Next thing you know, she's stuck with a lifetime of clothes shopping and epidurals.

Most of you read the story and think that this could never happen to you. You're smarter, savvier, better. Yet the story for many single Christians is exactly the same. The one thing you yearn for is not yours. But instead of hanging your hat on God's goodness, the same God who gave you every single blessing in your life, you choose to assume that God's goodness has skipped you, and just like Eve, you fall so quickly that you're not sure what hit you.

Underline the next sentence in your book: God is good all the time. It is His nature to be good. His character is good. He only does what is good. His goodness extends to you, even when you don't see it. His goodness overflows into your life even when you don't recognize it. He is good even when you don't feel it. Psalm 84:11 says, "No good thing does he withhold from those who walk uprightly."

Believe it. It's who He is.

2. God Is Always in Control

One of my favorite things about God is that He is always in control. He is the ER doctor who calmly brings the kid back to life without breaking a sweat. He is the surgeon who can stop a bleeding aorta without a single word. He is the president facing a war who quietly claims the victory.

But He's even more than that. He rules over evil. He controls the outcomes of every single situation in every single place. He is simply running the universe with His feet up.

He is not surprised by your singleness. He knows if you're ever going to get married and to whom.

God is always in control, no matter what seems to be

happening around you, and no matter how long you've been waiting. Nothing happens in your life without God allowing it. You can stop trying to make it to every singles meeting in the hopes of finally running into "the one"; you can cease striving and rest. God is in control. You can breathe now.

3. God Is Always Faithful

By now you know a lot about me. You know I'm far from perfect, so you can imagine how thankful I am for God's faithfulness. I am who I am today because of His faithfulness. Another favorite verse of mine is in 2 Timothy 2:13. Here's what it says: "If we are faithless, he remains faithful."

Can you get a hold of this truth? It's pretty incredible, given the mess you and I make of our lives. If you've been married before, you're probably acutely aware of the places in your life where you've failed. Even if you've never been married, it doesn't take long to see how often and how far your faithlessness extends. It's easy to lose hope and slowly drift away from the Lord.

What's amazing about God, among many things, is His utter faithfulness to us even when we don't deserve it.

WHAT'S AMAZING about God, among many things, is His utter faithfulness to us even when we don't deserve it.

I've been a follower of Christ for a long time now. I accepted Christ as my Savior when I was seven years old. It hit me one day that I've sinned a whole lot more since Christ came into my life than before He did. You can see where I'm going with this. It's easy to let guilt accumulate. Sinning when you don't know any better is one thing, but the longer I've walked with the Lord, the worse my sin feels because I ought to know better.

Over the years, I've been tempted to refuse God's faithfulness to me, not because I don't believe I need it, but because of the depth of my own depravity and faithlessness. How could I accept God's faithfulness, knowing how often I'd already asked for forgiveness, and fallen repeatedly in the same areas of sin? The last thing I want to be is a hypocrite. So sometimes, instead of running toward God's faithfulness, I've isolated myself and basked in my own shell of faithlessness.

You must stop believing the lie that God's faithfulness only reaches you as you improve. God wants you to come to Him just as you are. He is the One who cleanses you. You can't start the cleaning process yourself. That's His job. Your job is to humbly admit your need for Him.

God's faithfulness is complete and persistent toward us, even when we are faithless. Nothing will give you a greater sense of freedom than grasping the truth that God is faithful to you—all the time.

Now that's a truth to thrive on.

4. God Knows You Perfectly

I'll end with this fourth unbelievable character trait of God. He knows you inside and out. He knows you perfectly!

The fancy word for this trait is *omniscience*. God knows everything. He knows everything about you. He knows every thought you've ever had. He hears every unspoken prayer you've ever not uttered. He sees you. He knows you. He loves you.

I love Psalm 139. There are two verses in it that blow my mind away. The first is verse 4: "Even before a word is on my tongue, behold, O Lord, you know it altogether." The second is verse 16: "Your eyes saw my unformed substance; in your book were written, every one of them, the days that were formed for me, when as yet there was none of them." God formed you and made a plan for your life even before you became a zygote. He planned every aspect of your life. He knows you completely.

As a single Christian, nothing fills me with a greater sense of joy than understanding that I am known and loved completely by Jesus Christ. Satan wants you to believe the lie that if God really knew you and understood your needs, He would have provided a marriage partner for you.

Satan is a liar, and he only speaks lies. God's truth is clear: He knows you completely and He still loves you.

God's character is the anchor that allows every single Christian to thrive. Are you holding on to His character? You may have found true love in Christ when you accepted His gift of salvation. It's time for you to start trusting His character as you walk daily with Him.

As you hold on to God's character, you will be able to embrace the attitudes God wants you to live by and jump over the obstacles He so lovingly wants you to avoid.

Now that you know who God is, I think it's time you know God's plan for you.

GET ON GOD'S PROGRAM

You're on the road to discovering true love in Christ. You started with an understanding of Christ's sacrificial love for you. You then learned the truth about who God is. The truth of His character will carry you through your life, day in and day out. But God has even more for you to thrive.

God created you for relationship. The most important relationship is your vertical relationship with God through the perfect love of Christ. But that's not the only relationship God has given you. He has a perfect plan for every single Christian to grow in love and to thrive as you embrace His plan for your life.

I truly believe that this is where most single Christians get stuck. You get the God part down. You trust the Lord for salvation and hang on to who He is, but you have trouble understanding why God would have you live the rest of your life isolated and alone.

How could a God who says He loves relationship leave you on your own?

But God hasn't left you to live life alone. Life alone may be more comfortable and easy, especially on major family holidays, but it isn't God's plan for you.

Community and Relationship

God's plan for you is horizontal relationships with other people, within the context of the local church.

Whaaat? That's all you got? I'm not sure when the single Christian community became disenchanted with the local church, but it's not an uncommon sentiment. Some of you may be disappointed when you hear that God's solution to your horizontal love needs is found in the local church, but that could be because of your past experience with the local church.

I think it's time you get a biblical perspective on this issue.

The thing about Paul writing to the church in Corinth is that he knew all about the church: the good, the bad, and the ugly. But Paul also understood that God's plan for His people is fellowship and relationship within Christ's bride, the church.

GOD'S PLAN FOR you is horizontal relationships with other people, within the context of the local church.

Let's go all the way back to Acts 2:42–47. Peter had just preached the sermon of his lifetime. After 3,000 people turned to Christ, Peter got them together and a church was birthed. The first church had four elements that would feed the soul of believers, helping them to thrive:

1. They grew in their knowledge of God by studying His Word.
2. They maintained uncommon community through breaking of bread and prayer.
3. They developed meaningful relationships with each other through generosity and hospitality.
4. They worshiped God by lifting their voices in praise.

The early church in Acts didn't have singles groups and married groups and male and female groups. It didn't seek to accommodate the consumerist needs of its people. There was no mention of separation of people by demographics, geography, or hobbies.

The early church was primarily concerned with worshiping Jesus Christ and was known for its unity and sense of uncommon community.

The Corinthian church had deviated from the early church model, and Paul had to address the need for unity throughout his letter to the church. The early church model was the context that Paul wanted to bring back to the church in Corinth. And it is the context that every single Christian must strive toward in order to thrive.

Perhaps it's time you admit your disappointment with the church and let go of the growing chip on your shoulder. Get back on to God's program for you. God's people are not perfect (except for you and me, of course), but they are the family that God has given you. Love them and serve them for the sake of Christ.

WHAT DOES ALL THIS
MEAN TO THE SINGLE CHRISTIAN?

Shortly after I broke off my first engagement and was nursing a broken heart, I moved to a new city, took a new job, and had no friends.

I was Christian enough to find a good Bible-teaching church, but I lived forty minutes away from that church. It was a dark time in my life for a while. I felt alone and broken.

It didn't take long for me to understand that God loves

the brokenhearted. In the darkness of my apartment, God met me in ways I didn't see coming. In Hosea 2:14–15, God says this: "I will allure her, and bring her into the wilderness, and speak tenderly to her. And there I will give her her vineyards and make the Valley of Achor a door of hope."

I was thrown into a wilderness, but the Lord found me. I was in the valley of trouble, and I was given hope. Brokenness is the best place to be if you're looking to thrive. I was broken, but was well on my way toward the life that thrives.

Now all I had to do was figure out how to fit into my local church. Sunday after Sunday I showed up to church, sat in the third row, and left without as much as a word to anyone. My faith was growing as I fed on God's Word. My love for the Lord was burning, but I couldn't understand His people. Not only did I not connect with the church at large, but I didn't connect with the singles group either.

So I floundered for a few months. I questioned the Lord. I felt pretty sorry for myself. I thought of changing churches. I spent a lot of time scoping out churches on the web. I joined eHarmony for the first time.

NOT ONLY DID I not connect with the church at large, but I didn't connect with the singles group either.

And still I felt alone and isolated in a church designed for couples.

One day, as I sat in my room and prayed, a funny thought crossed my mind. *What if instead of waiting for others to talk to me at church, I took the initiative and talked to them? What if instead of being ministered to and led, I took it upon myself to minister to others?*

I certainly knew the Lord well enough to serve in His church, and I was slowly but surely learning to trust His unwavering character. What did I have to lose?

The next Sunday I did it. I actually talked to the person to my right. I participated in the Sunday school class. A few weeks later I shared my testimony in a Bible study. Next thing I knew, I was being asked to teach a tiny (five people) women's Bible study.

Me? Teach a Bible study? I was the least likely person qualified to do it. Yet God often reminds me that His plans are way different than mine, but they're always for my best!

I did teach the class and to everyone's surprise, and mostly to mine, it was good. It wasn't long before I felt God calling me to full-time ministry. Fifteen years later, here you are, reading my story.

I went through my story all over again to tell you this: there will come a time in your life as a single Christian when you must stop looking to be ministered to and start ministering to others. There will come a time in your life when you must intentionally and prayerfully forget about your program, and get on God's program instead. That may mean it's time for you to join a Bible study. It could also mean that you speak up and get authentic with fellow Christians. It could even mean doing something so completely out of your comfort zone, like starting a new ministry with little experience and knowledge and absolute dependence on the Lord, and seeing Him bear fruit.

It could mean simply loving someone in need.

God's program is for uncommon community with other believers. Uncommon community is not perfect, but it is Christlike in its authenticity and grace. The answer to your relationship needs is not for God to magically provide the perfect partner for you, although He could do that in a heartbeat.

Your relationship needs are first met in Christ and then grown as you live your life in true fellowship with other believers. That's where you will find relationship. That's where you will find accountability. That's where you will find victory. Are you in fellowship with other believers? I know the church is not perfect, but for better or for worse, it's Christ's bride, and it's God's plan for your life today.

If you want to know what love is, you must start with finding true love in Christ, but you must then quickly move on to loving others, no matter how much or how little you may like them. Without Christ's love filling you and guiding you, you cannot thrive. But when you draw on Christ's love, everything else will come.

12

Hit the Road Jack: Executing the Life That Thrives

People always want to know how hard it was for me to break off my engagements. They admire my boldness and courage. They want to know my secret. I tell them it was easy. Once I made up my mind, the secret was in acting quickly and firmly before I changed my mind.

Most people talk about doing something but rarely take action. By the time they muster the courage to do something, they find that it's too late, and the feeling has passed. I vividly remember the first broken engagement: my ex-fiancé walking out of my apartment, diamond ring in hand, leaving me in the wake of the aftermath.

I put personal feelings aside, got on the phone, and canceled the caterer, florist, and chapel. Then I called key people who would be flying into town two weeks from that moment, and I broke the news gently but firmly to them. I was thankful for answering machines on that surprisingly sunny fall morning in Houston. I then walked down to the office of my apartment complex and told the nice Texan lady that

I wouldn't be needing the two-bedroom apartment after all (that I had *just* moved into). At this point, I finally broke down in tears in front of the nice Texan lady.

If there's one thing I've learned in life it's that feelings are terrible leaders, but they make excellent followers. Change happens when you know exactly what you need to do. In an act of your will, take a step of action whether you feel like it or not. It is only then that you will see the pieces falling into place.

I hope that by this point in the book, you understand that God's plan for every single Christian is to thrive. No more languishing in self-pity. No more rotting in bitterness. No more loss of self-control, and no more haphazard holiness. You were made for more.

That doesn't mean that you won't get married or that you should give up on the notion of getting married. It just means that God's will for your life exceeds marriage as we know it. You were made for more.

I also hope that by now you have a clearer understanding of God's love for you and His plan for your life. Now it's time to determine, by an act of your will, to do something about all the things you've learned, or else you'll be just another single Christian who's read a relatively decent book on singleness with lots of references to sex in it.

In other words, it's time to hit the road running. It's time to take action. Let's first spend a few moments looking at the lame excuses you will face as you proceed on the road to thrive.

KILLING YOUR LAME EXCUSES

Excuses, excuses, excuses. You have bags full of excuses. Instead of suffocating under the weight of your excuses, let's try to identify and kill some of the most common excuses that you will come up with to keep from thriving.

1. I Don't Have Enough Time

Time is an interesting commodity. It stretches forever when you're waiting for vacation, but flies by when you're *on* vacation. Thirty minutes feel like an eternity when you're pushing out a baby, but like a blink when you're on your first date with your latest crush. Lack of time is one of the primary excuses that single Christians use when it comes to embracing the life that thrives.

Who has time to go to church and build relationships with others?

Who has time to study God's character and jump on His program?

I am pretty busy. I'm one of the busiest people I know. I work as a pediatric emergency doctor and I am the women's ministry director at my church of several thousand people. I write a daily blog and pick up random other writing projects along the way—like this book. I speak on a regular basis, and I try to exercise five times a week. I'm not bragging; by now, we all know how dumb I can actually be, but I often get asked what I do to keep my head above water with my busy schedule.

I WANT PASSION without drive, focus without insensitivity.

What I start by telling people is that the goal in life isn't simply to be busy. I happen to be in a busy season of my life, but that is not something to strive for. Remember that your goal is to thrive whether you're busy or not. I want deep and meaningful relationships in my life. I want to avoid the sense of frenzy and restlessness. I want a real prayer life and greater intimacy with Jesus. I want passion without drive, focus without insensitivity.

I also have exactly the same number of hours in a day as you do, and have found that these principles have helped me thrive, despite a hectic lifestyle:

I don't do everything. It's true. I don't. Because I need time to develop the attitudes that will help me thrive, I automatically have to rule out certain habits that will consume the hours of my day and leave me breathless. So I don't date as much as the next person does, and I don't watch as many movies as everybody else does. I accept the fact that I must first do the things that will help my soul to thrive.

I multitask when I can. If you're a single mom, you're very familiar with multitasking. Though multitasking is not for everyone, it certainly has its advantages. I tend to memorize Scripture when I'm on the treadmill, and I listen to the Bible while I water my plants. I look for ways to feed my soul with activities that will cause me to thrive, whenever I can.

I maintain an organized and disciplined lifestyle. Discipline is an art that is learned with time, and it grows with practice. If you want to make the most of the twenty-four hours in your day, get disciplined. Wake up early, go to bed on time, and plan your days well. You will find you'll be able to do twice as much as you used to.

Every single Christian has the same twenty-four hours in the day, and the same seven days in the week, and the same 365 days in the year, with an extra day to catch up every four years. Isn't it time you kill this lame excuse and find the time to thrive?

2. I Don't Have Enough Money

It was Paul who said in 1 Timothy 6:10 that "the love of money is a root of all kinds of evils." While you may not think you love money, if you think you can't thrive without a certain amount of money, then you may be more in love with money than you think.

I used to think that marriage would double my income and allow me to do more for the Lord, plus I'd get a better tax break. Then I realized that most married people have kids, which means they have the added expenses of clothes, schools, babysitters, doctor visits, ballet, soccer, piano, college, among the many other expenses that families run into.

If you're a single parent, I can hear your objections right now.

"But, but, but, you don't understand how hard it is for me. I have to work two jobs, I can barely afford my mortgage. I don't have money for babysitters. I'm too broke to thrive. Frankly, I'm too afraid to thrive."

I believe the plight of the single mom is not an easy one, especially if you've found yourself in a situation where the father is not an active participant in the financial or physical upbringing of your kids. It's easy to wonder where God is when your bills are stacking up and no one at your church seems to notice.

If you identify with the picture of the single Christian who is unable to thrive due to financial constraints, let me once again review these principles for you right now:

God is your Provider. Let's go back once more to my favorite Bible story from Genesis 16. Abraham and Sarah had tried for years to have a child but couldn't. Sarah gets the genius idea to use Sarah's servant, Hagar, to have an heir for Abraham. Hagar, the maid who really couldn't say no to her master, ends up pregnant. Of course, when she does, Sarah becomes jealous and kicks her out of the house.

HE UNDERSTANDS her predicament. He lovingly reminds her that He is near, and that He sees her.

In Genesis 16 we find Hagar alone in the wilderness, pregnant, in utter despair, the furthest thing from thriving as you can possibly imagine. And it is in this state of fear and despair that God finds Hagar and meets her in her point of need. God knows exactly what Hagar is going through. He understands her predicament. He lovingly reminds her that He is near, and that He sees her. Hagar is so moved that she calls the place where she meets God *Beer-lahai-roi* or, "the God who sees." And she returns to Abraham as God instructed her to do, ready to thrive.

If you're finding yourself alone in a wilderness and very little in this book has touched you thus far, I hope Hagar's story is a turning point for you. God's love extends to you and He sees you no matter where you are or why you've ended up in your wilderness.

You don't need a lot of money to thrive. You simply need a new perspective. God has promised to provide for your needs. In Philippians 4:19, Paul reminds us that "my God will supply every need of yours according to his riches in glory in Christ Jesus."

Will you embrace it and choose to live by faith?

3. I Don't Know Enough People

Your excuse may not be related to time or money. Your excuse may simply be that you're new in town and don't know enough people to thrive. Because you're alone, you end up spending way too much time in front of the computer and eventually see things you shouldn't be seeing. Or maybe you get lost in love stories and romance-based novels, fantasizing about life as it should be, leading to a mindset of discontentment and lack of joy.

I find that the older I get, the harder it is to make close friends, and the greater the challenge it is to find the life that thrives. Though I've already discussed loneliness to a greater extent earlier in the book, here are three simple things you can do to develop relationship in your life:

Be proactive at church. After two years of attending a wonderful church in Chicago, I noticed that I hardly knew anyone and felt lost in the shuffle of a huge church. I also struggled to find my place in the ministry I thought God had called me to. After much prayer, I mustered the courage to set up a meeting with the women's ministry director and express my interest in getting involved. I told her I'd be willing to do anything, as long as I could be used by God to serve His people. Trust me, that director was more than happy to take me up on my offer, and she is now one of my best friends. In fact, a few years later, I found myself directing the women's ministry at that same church as it grew to become a multicampus church. While your story may not turn out exactly like mine, there comes a point in your life when you must stop waiting for people to notice you, humble yourself, and be proactive in reaching out to others.

Be present at singles meetings. When I complain about not dating, my friend Lynda, who helps run the singles ministry, reminds me that she has never once seen me at a singles meeting. Though my initial response is that I don't have time, I quickly kill that lame excuse and nod my head in agreement. She's right. And you won't develop relationships (male or female) if you don't start hanging around other people.

Be hospitable at home. My pastor likes to say that you don't need a big budget to be hospitable—a bag of Doritos and a six-pack of Diet Coke will do. He's right. The best way to get to know people is to invite them over to your home. When was the last time you went out on a limb, put away your own insecurities, and had some people over? I bet you're thinking your house is too small, or your roommate won't allow it. Hospitality is biblical. Pray for it, then take a step of faith and do it!

If you follow these three simple ways to meet people, you'll soon find that your life is bursting with thriving relationships.

4. I Don't Know Where to Start

I'll confess that this one is not a lame excuse. It's a true fear that you will face as you're making some basic changes in your life.

Sometimes patients come into the doctor's office overweight with high blood pressure, high cholesterol, and a history of smoking. They know they have a problem, but they have no idea how to fix it.

A good doctor will not tell patients to just forget about it because the problem is too hard to fix. That's dumb. No, a good doctor will instruct the patient to pick one thing, anything, do it, and then do the next thing. You don't have to do it all in one day. Break it down into achievable goals. Make a list. I love lists. You won't see immediate results right away, but you will eventually see results.

There is an old Chinese proverb that says, "A journey of a thousand miles begins with a single step." I agree. The Christian life that thrives is not a race to be run in a day; it is a lifelong journey of increasing growth and dependence on the Lord Jesus Christ.

NO "ONE SIZE FITS ALL"

There are four kinds of singles reading this book: the "never married and never want to" single, the "never married but want to" single, "the once married and never again" single, or the "once married and hope to again" single. You probably can think of at least two or three other categories, but the point I'm trying to make is that there is no "one size fits all" road to thriving.

Your road to thriving will depend on where you've been and where you're headed. As a child of God, you're headed heavenward. And though every child of God is ultimately headed to the same place, the road you're on will not look exactly like my road. As a now middle-aged, twice-engaged virgin, the bags I've got to work through will look drastically different than yours if you're an eighteen-year-old, right-out-of-high-school prom queen.

And that's okay.

THERE IS NO "one size fits all" road to thriving.

I love the passage in Luke 13:6–9. The passage is a parable that Jesus tells the Galileans.

"A man had a fig tree planted in his vineyard, and he came seeking fruit on it and found none. And he said to the vinedresser, 'Look, for three years now I have come seeking fruit on this fig tree, and I find none. Cut it down. Why should it use up the ground?' And he answered him, 'Sir, let it alone this year also, until I dig around it and put on manure. Then if it should bear fruit next year, well and good; but if not, you can cut it down.'"

You may be wondering what this parable has to do with the single life that thrives. I'm about to give you four principles from this parable that will help you as you're executing the life that thrives.

1. It's Never Too Late to Thrive

In this beautiful parable, the man and the vinedresser are looking at the same fig tree, but they see two different things. The man sees a dying tree ready to be cut down. The vinedresser with ever-patient eyes sees a tree with huge potential for thriving. If you haven't picked up on it yet, the vinedresser is a picture of our Lord. He never gives up on us. It's never too late for us to thrive. If you've counted yourself out because you can't see the figs on your branches, just wait. Thriving isn't about you. It's about the expertise of the vinedresser. Give the Vinedresser room to do His work, and pretty soon, you'll see that you too will bear fruit and thrive.

2. Thriving Takes Time

The vinedresser promises figs, but he needs a year to produce them. Too many single Christians want immediate results, and if you don't see it right now, you quickly want to give up. This parable is a reminder that fruit grows over time. I'm not much of a gardener, and I've been tempted to give up on my plants way too soon. God, the Vinedresser, is a perfect gardener, and He knows exactly where to prune you and what to purge in order to produce a life that thrives. Are you willing to give Him the time to do His best work in you?

3. It's Not the Number of Figs, but the Presence of Figs

The way you can tell whether a fig tree is thriving is by the presence of figs on the tree. Consider ten different fig trees. Some of them may have five figs on their branches, while others will have ten figs on them. It's not the number of figs but the presence of figs that indicate that a tree is thriving. It's the same way with your life, single Christian. Your fruitfulness and your thriving will look different from your friend's. So stop judging your life by how others are doing. What the Vinedresser cares about is increasing fruitfulness. Give Him time, and don't judge your life too soon.

4. Thriving Demands You Use Your Manure

My favorite part in this parable is the part where the vinedresser tells the man to put manure on the dying tree. Whatever you think stinks most in your life right now is the very thing God will use to grow your tree. If you feel like you have a lot of manure in your life, don't worry. God will use that manure to bring forth much fruit. Do you need more figs on your tree? Be willing to allow God to use your manure. That's a little known secret of the life that thrives. Trust me, I know about manure; my life has been full of it, but God is using every bit of it for His glory.

WHATEVER YOU think stinks most in your life right now is the very thing God will use to grow your tree.

And I praise Him for it. Remember that if you're in Christ, you're headed heavenward, but how you get there is up to the Vinedresser.

Are you ready to kill your lame excuses in order to live the life that thrives? Are you ready to get on with your life, expecting much fruit? Are you ready to hit the road, Jack?

I hope you are, because whether you know it or not, if you're in Christ, you are on the road to thrive.

Conclusion
Not Just Pie in the Sky: Real-Life Examples of Thriving

They say talk is cheap. I tend to agree (even though I like to talk a lot). We have just spent a lot of time talking. It's easy to think that all this talk about thriving is pie-in-the-sky, lofty Christianese. But does anybody actually live this way?

I'd like to spend this last chapter telling you about some real-life examples of people whose lives have thrived. You may recognize many of the names. I've greatly abbreviated each story due to space constraints and the purposes of this book. Many of these men and women have impacted my life greatly in my pursuit of a thriving life. I hope you will find them a joy and an encouragement to your life.

As our journey together comes to a close, I have a couple of thoughts to add. First of all, I hope I don't get married next week. I remember reading *I Kissed Dating Goodbye* and finding out that the author, Joshua Harris, got married shortly after the release of the book. I was slightly disappointed for some sick reason. I worry that the message of this book will be lessened if I marry, but they say that a comet passes only every ten years or so, so I'm pretty sure the odds are still in my favor to remain single for a while.

The second thing I would like you to know is that even though I've never met you, I have loved you in every page of this book. I will miss you, my fellow sojourner. Only eternity in heaven will fully tell the stories of our thriving. The single Christian life is not easy. May God give us the grace to continue to reflect His light to a world in need of a Savior.

May your undivided devotion to Jesus Christ be fully rewarded here on this earth and throughout eternity. May you find in Christ a friendship so deep that nothing can break it, and a companion so near that nothing can stand in the way. May your likeness to Jesus Christ be obvious to those who look carefully.

And now it is my joy to introduce you to these amazing Christians whose lives have blazed in love for Jesus Christ, our Lord and Savior, whose name be glorified both now and forever.

There is no greater joy than to thrive for His glory.

REAL-LIFE EXAMPLES

David Brainerd (1718–1747)

Missionary to the Indians.
Engaged but never married.

———— ❖ ————

"I have received my all from God.
Oh that I could return my all to God."[29]

W ho would think that a man who spent most of his adult life plagued with illness (one that would lead to his death at twenty-nine years of age) would make the list of single Christians who thrived? Yet David Brainerd leads the list with his unparalleled devotion to the Lord throughout his brief life.

David was born, in Connecticut and the sixth of nine children, to a poor Christian family. David's father died when he was only nine, and his mother when he was fourteen. He came to know the Lord Jesus Christ at the age of twenty-one. That year he started his studies at Yale University but became sick with tuberculosis. He managed to return to Yale, where a spiritual awakening was happening as a result of George Whitefield's preaching. David fit right in, as he too was passionate about life in Christ. Shortly afterwards, when David was twenty-three years old, Ebenezer Pembertson, a famous preacher, visited Yale and gave a moving account of the need for missionary work to the Indians. David, barely healthy, vowed "to be wholly the Lord's, to be forever devoted to His service."[30]

Trouble has a way of quickly following big steps of obedience to the Lord. David would soon be expelled from Yale for criticizing a tutor. Though he sought forgiveness later, the school authorities wouldn't reinstate him. David was devastated but could only fast and pray, seeking to find out how the Lord would still wholly use him in undivided devotion for Him.

He was licensed to preach and became an itinerant preacher for some months until Pemberton called him to discuss ministering to the Indians in the Northeast. David's health was still deteriorating at that time, and he could hardly preach an entire sermon standing up, yet at age twenty-five, he accepted the call to become a missionary to the Indians.

David Brainerd would spend only four years ministering to the Indians until he finally succumbed to the ravages of TB. These four years were not easy. His health was not improving, and he often traveled alone on foot, heavy and despondent. He faced a huge language barrier with the Indians. But David Brainerd prayed. And the more he prayed, the more God worked.

By his twenty-ninth birthday, David Brainerd had eighty-five true converts among the Indians. By then, he had nothing left in him. He died in the house of the great preacher Jonathan Edwards, being cared for by Jerusha Edwards, to whom he had become engaged but never married. She too died a few months later, having contracted the same illness as David's.

It's easy to wonder how such a short life would be considered a life that thrived. David didn't build any great buildings or write any great books, but he did keep a journal. This journal would later be used by Jonathan Edwards to publish a small book about the life of David Brainerd. This book would have tremendous results and would greatly influence some of the greatest Christians of this century—men like William Carey, John Wesley, Robert McCheyne, Henry Martyn, Jim Elliot, John Piper, and many, many others.

David Brainerd's life may seem wasted from the perspective of this world, but from God's perspective, his was a life that thrived for the utmost of God's glory.

Amy Carmichael (1867–1951)

Missionary to India.
Founder of the Donhavur Fellowship,
a society devoted to saving neglected
and ill-treated children.
Never married.

"You can give without loving,
but you cannot love without giving."[31]

She may be the poster child for the single Christian woman who thrived, but Amy Carmichael was much more than that. She was a missionary to India and started an orphanage that, over time, cared for thousands of children. She served in India for fifty-six years without furlough and has written too many books to list.

Amy was the oldest of seven children, born to a devout Presbyterian family in Northern Ireland. She spent three years in boarding school until her parents couldn't afford it anymore. Her father died shortly after her sixteenth birthday. She was then brought up by Robert Wilson, the cofounder of the Keswick Convention, a Christian missionary organization. It was there, at age twenty, that she heard Hudson Taylor speak about missionary life and soon became convinced that God had called her to missions. She was an unlikely candidate for mission work, as she suffered from neuralgia that made her weak and gave her frequent episodes of uncontrollable pain; in those times of pain, she was bedridden.

She initially spent fifteen months in Japan before being moved to what would become her lifelong call in India. Her work in India was mainly with young girls who Amy removed from forced prostitution. She founded the Donhavur Fellowship as a place of safety for over one thousand children she helped save.

At age sixty-four, Amy had a horrible fall that caused her to be bedridden until her death almost twenty years later. How could God still use Amy, who remained bedridden for the final twenty years of her life? She wrote over thirty-five books to her credit, inspiring many people, like Elisabeth Elliot and myself.

Amy didn't want a gravestone at her death. Instead, the children of Donhavur put a bird bath over her grave with the word *Amma* on it, which means "Mother" in their dialect. Though Amy never married nor had any children of her own, she had many more children calling her "Mother" than any of us would ever dream of.

Amy's life is a sobering reminder that the life that thrives does not depend on great circumstances but on the steady presence of the Lord Jesus Christ, who never leaves us nor forsakes us.

Mary Slessor (1848–1915)

"White Queen of Calabar"
Missionary on the west coast of Africa.
Never married.

"Lord, the task is impossible for me, but not for
Thee. Lead the way and I will follow."[32]

Mary Slessor was born in Scotland to a very poor family. Her father was a drunk, her mother a godly woman. At age eleven, Mary was earning a living by working in factories twelve hours a day, six days a week.

As a young child, Mary had given her life to Jesus, thanks to the influence of her mother. In 1874, news of David Livingstone's death shook the land and created an increased interest in missions, especially missions to Africa. Mary was one of those whose heart was stirred. She, like David Livingstone, had taught herself to read. At age twenty-eight, she was on her way to Africa to join a small mission station along the Calabar, on the west coast of Africa. This was a dangerous area known as "White Man's Grave." Slavery was common; violence and cruelty were the norm.

It didn't take long for Mary to get settled in her hut at one of the outlying villages and start the work God had called her to. Though she had never gone to school herself, Mary still spent her time teaching, speaking, and nursing the sick. When she spoke, the people gathered to listen. In a land of death, she brought the message of life.

After her work along the coast flourished, Mary was thankful but not satisfied. Her heart longed to reach the interior of the jungle, among the cannibals, where people desperately needed the good news of the gospel. Despite many discouraging her from going to these unreached areas, Mary got in a canoe and went "forward and onward." This would always be her motto in serving the Lord.

God blessed her courage, and her work saw hundreds of lives changed and a number of churches birthed. Mary often fought tropical diseases and great dangers, but her indomitable spirit never wavered. God had called her, and He would sustain her.

Mary Slessor was undaunted by loneliness, fear, and sickness. She decided to follow Jesus no turning back, no turning back. Her life counted for the kingdom of God.

Helen Roseveare (1925–)

Medical Missionary to the Congo.
Speaker.
Author.
Engaged once but never married.

"If Christ be God and died for me,
then no sacrifice can be too
great for me to make for Him."[33]

Helen Roseveare was born in England in 1925. She was very well educated and became a follower of Jesus Christ while studying at Cambridge. She continued to pursue a medical education with the goal of becoming a missionary doctor.

After receiving her medical degree at age twenty-eight, she headed for the Congo to begin her work in the mission field. Helen was extremely intelligent and efficient, but her role as a woman created a struggle with other missionaries and nationals. Her dream was to train locals in nursing skills and the Word of God so that they in turn could reach out to their own people, thus expanding the work. The local missionaries didn't agree with Helen's vision to train the nationals in medical skills.

Despite the conflict, within two years Helen had built a training center and had four graduates who had passed the government medical exams. Her colleagues still were not impressed, and sent Helen into an old leprosy camp in the jungle to start a new work from scratch. This was a difficult blow for Helen who had already spent so much of herself in the training center, but she would remain focused and undeterred.

She built another hospital from scratch and resumed her training of African nurses. Sadly, Helen remained a threat to her male colleagues, and the missionary organization would soon send a man and his wife to oversee the work that was already going so well under Helen's supervision. This was devastating to Helen, who had been her own boss for far too long and found it difficult to submit to this imposed leadership. After over a year of struggling for control, she left the Congo for furlough, disillusioned and defeated.

In England, Helen became convinced that many of her problems with the male missionaries were the result of her not having a husband. She soon went about the task of finding a male doctor suitable to marry her. She prayed that God would answer her request, or else she wouldn't go back to Africa. She had a minimakeover, found a young man who would fit the bill, but at the last minute, the plans fell through as he couldn't go through with it. He simply didn't love Helen enough.

Helen was sorely disappointed and still single at thirty-five, but by now was starting to recognize that she was attempting to accomplish her will without God. She adjusted her perspective and soon would return to the Congo alone, ready to resume the work God had called her to. By that time, there was much political unrest in the Congo, and many of the missionaries had left the country for their safety. Helen felt that if God had called her to Africa, He would protect her. So she stayed.

This was a time of great growth for Helen, who was learning to trust the Lord more and more and see His hand in every detail of her life. She recognized her own sinfulness and lack of dependence on the Lord. "I was unable to reach the standard I myself had set, let alone God's. Try as I would, I met only frustration in this longing to achieve, to be worthy."[34]

There was worse to come. As the rebels in the Congo gained strength, Helen was taken into captivity for five months and later, in an attempt to escape, was raped by a group of soldiers. Instead of shriveling in bitterness, God used this event in Helen's life to minister to other single missionaries who had also lost their purity at the hands of violence and rape. Her relationship with the Lord remained undamaged.

In 1964, at the age of thirty-nine, Helen was finally rescued from the Congo. Helen returned once more to the Congo for a seven-year stint, but by then the work was not the same. When she left the Congo for good, it was in disappointment and a sense of futility. She went through a period of deep loneliness where all she could do was turn to the Lord, whose presence remained and fed her soul. Little did she know that God still had great plans for Helen. She soon became involved in an entirely new ministry as a very successful international speaker for foreign missions.

Helen has also authored several books. Her testimony depicts the life of a woman who thrived despite many setbacks and seeming defeat, reminding us that we don't have to be perfect to thrive for the Lord; we simply have to be surrendered.

Henrietta Mears (1890–1963)

Christian educator in Hollywood, California.
Sunday school teacher.
Author of Sunday school curriculum.
Founder of retreat center for youth.
Never married.

———— ❖ ————

"God doesn't call us to sit on
the sidelines and watch. He calls us
to be on the field, playing the games."[35]

Henrietta Mears was born the youngest of seven children in Fargo, North Dakota, in 1890. She soon grew in her devotion to the Lord under the heavy influence of her mother.

As a child, doctors told her mother that Henrietta would be blind by the age of thirty. Convinced that God had a specific purpose for her life, Henrietta read and studied all the more to prepare her for losing her eyesight. She graduated from the University of Minnesota with honors, having found her gift for teaching. Though she had extreme nearsightedness during her life, she never fully lost her vision, but was constantly dependent on the Lord because of it.

After a few years of teaching, at the age of thirty, Henrietta accepted a position as Director of Christian Education at the First Presbyterian Church of Hollywood, California. This position would change her life forever. The Sunday school attendance quickly went from 450 to 4,000 within two years, due to Henrietta's influence. She rewrote the curriculum that was soon in demand by other churches.

As more demand for her curriculum came in, Henrietta started Gospel Light International, a publishing company. She also founded the Forest Home Conference Center that offered young people a beautiful setting where they could learn the Bible.

Her passion was to spread the gospel and train future leaders. She influenced many great leaders including Bill Bright, who founded the Campus Crusade for Christ, and Billy Graham, who said about her, "I doubt if any other woman outside my wife and mother has had such a marked influence on my life. She is certainly one of the greatest Christians I have ever known."[36]

She was well known for her flamboyant hats and colorful accessories but mostly for her love of the Lord Jesus Christ and His Word. Though she never married, she has had hundreds of spiritual children. Only heaven will reveal the full harvest of fruitfulness that the thriving life will reap for God's kingdom.

Gladys Aylward (1902–1970)

Missionary to China.
Never married.

"I wasn't God's first choice for what I've done for
China. There was somebody else. I don't know
who it was—God's first choice. It must have
been a man—a wonderful man, a well-educated
man. I don't know what happened. Perhaps he
died. Perhaps he wasn't willing. And God
looked down and saw Gladys Aylward."[37]

Gladys Aylward was born to a poor family in London in
1902, was very small in stature, and became a parlor
maid at the age of fourteen. One day, on her way home from
church, a stranger confronted her with the gospel.

Gladys began to develop a love for China while reading
the many books on China that she found in the library of her
employers. By the time she applied to the mission board at
age twenty-eight, she was thought to be too old and unfit to
learn the Chinese language and was rejected. Though initially crushed, she figured if she couldn't go with the mission
board, she would go alone. She saved her money each month
until she had enough for a one-way train ticket to China.

She began the journey to China at the age of thirty, alone
and determined. She joined a veteran missionary and helped
in running an inn for mule drivers. She learned the Chinese
language while interacting with the mule drivers. After

the veteran missionary she was working with passed away, Gladys could not sustain the inn financially. At that time, the government asked her to be a foot inspector. This new job position required travel, and she used that opportunity to share Bible stories in the many new towns and villages she visited.

Gladys integrated so well with the Chinese people and culture that she remained there during the Japanese bombing of China in 1937. At one point, she even became a spy for the Chinese army. She began adopting war orphans during that time, and soon had close to one hundred children in her care.

She served in China for twenty years before returning to England. By then she had become somewhat of a celebrity in England, with a book and a movie made about her life. The movie embarrassed Gladys as she was played by Ingrid Bergman and was portrayed in fictional love scenes. Gladys was a chaste woman of God who remained single throughout her life, proclaiming the good news of the gospel to the people of China.

Gladys Aylward loved God and loved people. Her life is a strong example that love is the essential ingredient for the life that thrives.

Corrie ten Boom (1892–1983)

War hero.
Protector of the Jewish people.
Fell in love once, never married.

"There is no pit so deep that He is not deeper still."[38] (first quoted by Betsie ten Boom)

Corrie was born the youngest of four in a loving Christian home in Holland. Her father was a watchmaker who feared the Lord. She accepted Christ into her heart at the age of fourteen, and at sixteen, pondered what she would do next.

She became the first female watchmaker in Holland and remained unmarried. She did, however, experience a broken heart at the young age of twenty-three. She tells about it in her book *Tramp for the Lord*. Here's what she says:

I had to fight a battle over it. I was twenty-three. I loved a boy and believed he loved me. But I had no money, and he married a rich girl. After they were married he brought her to me and putting her hand in mine said, "I hope you two will be friends." I wanted to scream. She looked so sweet, so secure and content in his love.

But I did have Jesus, and eventually I went to Him and prayed, "Lord Jesus, You know that I belong to You 100 percent. My sex life is Yours also. I

265

don't know what plans You have for my life, but Lord, whatever it may be, use me to realize Your victory in every detail. I believe You can take away all my frustrations and feelings of unhappiness. I surrender anew my whole life to You."[39]

God certainly had plans for Corrie ten Boom. By the time the Second World War had begun, the Ten Booms were living a quiet life, working in the watchmaker's shop. When they saw the suffering of the Jews, they could not deny their faith, and their home became a hiding place for the Jews. The work lasted until 1944 when fifty-two-year-old Corrie, her sister Betsie, and their father were arrested and taken to Ravensbruck, one of Hitler's concentration camps. Betsie and their father would die in the concentration camp, but Corrie was released on New Year's Day in 1945, due to a clerical error. All women her age had been scheduled for execution.

Corrie spent the rest of her life traveling as an evangelist, speaker, and social advocate, telling the story of her life and God's love. She wrote several books, including her story in a book called *The Hiding Place.*

If you don't think you can thrive for the Lord after a broken heart, read Corrie ten Boom's story again. Hers is a life that understood that God's plan for the single Christian goes far beyond love and marriage. God's plan for the single Christian is the life that thrives.

Audrey Wetherell Johnson (1907–1984)

Founder of Bible Study Fellowship International.
Never married.

"My aim had always been to ensure that every
member of the class was living by the reading of
God's Word. God gave me a profound conviction
that the way to know Him intimately as a Person
related to me was through study of His Word
with the help of the Holy Spirit."[40]

Audrey Johnson was born in England in a Christian home, and accepted Christ as a child under the strong teaching of the Bible.

She spent years as a missionary to China, where she was imprisoned for some time. She eventually was able to go back to England for a brief furlough, but soon returned to China to teach the Bible at a seminary. The Chinese government placed under house arrest for eighteen months. She was forced to leave China permanently in 1950.

It was soon after that she found herself in the United States and was asked to teach five women who were already well-instructed in God's Word. Here she was, after years of serving the Lord in a real mission field, now being asked to teach the Bible to a meager five women? She initially struggled with the idea, but she quickly remembered Jeremiah 45:5 that says, "Do you seek great things for yourself? Seek them not."

She agreed to teach those five ladies, and little did she know that it was the beginning of Bible Study Fellowship International. Today BSF offers over one thousand Bible study classes in six continents. Audrey Johnson believed that by carefully studying the Word of God, people would come to know and trust God, who gives daily provisions and loving kindness. Too many people to count would agree with Audrey, as their lives are a living testimony of the impact that BSF has had on our modern-day church and culture.

One life, one Bible study, one person's willingness to humbly do the job that God gives, and the effect is priceless. That's the sum of the life that thrives for God's glory.

Notes

1. United States Census Bureau, "Unmarried and Single Americans Week Sept. 16–22, 2012," accessed July 2012, www.census.gov /newsroom/releases/archives/facts_for_features_special_editions /cb12-ff18.html.

2. Wikipedia, "Eunuch," November 20, 2012, accessed November 2012, en.wikipedia.org/wiki/Eunuch.

3. Anthony DeMello, *Chicken Soup for the Soul at Work: 101 Stories of Courage, Compassion and Creativity in the Workplace*, compiled by Jack L. Canfield, et al. (Deerfield Beach, FL: Health Communications, Inc., 1996), 310.

4. "Saturday Night (Is the Loneliest Night of the Week)," © 1944 by Sammy Cahn and Jule Styne (New York: Columbia Records).

5. Dictionary.com, LLC, "Let" definition, accessed July 2012, www. dictionary.reference.com/browse/let?s=t.

6. Dictionary.com, LLC, "Self-Control" definition, accessed July 2012, www.dictionary.reference.com/browse/self-control.

7. John Piper, "The Fierce Fruit of Self-Control," *desiringGod*, May 15, 2001, accessed July 2012, www.desiringgod.org/resource-library /taste-see-articles/the-fierce-fruit-of-self-control.

8. Michael Reece, et al., "Sexual Behaviors, Relationships, and Perceived Health among Adult Men in the United States: Results from a National Probability Sample," *Journal of Sexual Medicine* 7, Suppl. 5 (October 2010): 291–304.

9. Harold Leitenberg, Mark J. Detzer, and Debra Srebnik, "Gender Differences in Masturbation and the Relation of Masturbation Experience in Preadolescence and/or Early Adolescence to Sexual Behavior and Sexual Adjustment in Young Adulthood," *Archives of Sexual Behavior* 22 (April 1993): 87–98. Sample was 280 respondents from two "Introduction to Psychology" classes.

10. Lisa Ling, "The Evolution of Porn and Erotica," *Oprah*, November 17, 2009, accessed July 2012, www.oprah.com/relationships /Lisa-Ling-Reports-on-Adult-Films-Porn-and-Erotica.

11. Tyler Charles, "(Almost) Everyone's Doing It," *Relevant* Magazine, September/October 2011, accessed July 2012, www.relevant magazine.com/life/relationships/almost-everyones-doing-it.

12. John Piper, *Future Grace: The Purifying Power of Living by Faith in . . .* (Sisters, OR; Multnomah, 1995), 336.

13. Oswald Chambers, "Destiny of Holiness," accessed September 2012, www.oswaldchambers.co.uk/Readings.php?day=1&month =9&year=2012&language=English.

14. C. S. Lewis, *The Weight of Glory* (New York: HarperCollins, 1991), 26.

15. "Take My Life" © 1999 by Vineyard Music.

16. Dictionary.com, LLC, "Strive," accessed July 2012, www.dictionary .reference.com/browse/strive?s=t.

17. Dictionary.com, LLC, "Anxiety," accessed July 2012, www.dictionary .reference.com/browse/anxiety?s=t.

18. John Piper, "We Want You to Be a Christian Hedonist! *desiringGod,* August 31, 2006, accessed July 2012, www.desiringgod.org /resource-library/articles/we-want-you-to-be-a-christian-hedonist.

19. Sara Radicati, "Email Statistics Report, 2011–2015," The Radicati Group, Inc, May 2011, accessed July 2012, www.radicati.com /wp/wp-content/uploads/2011/05/Email-Statistics-Report-2011- 2015-Executive-Summary.pdf.

20. Doug Dickerson, "Running in Circles—A Leaders Guide to Musical Chairs," *Salem-News.com,* May 11, 2010, accessed November 2012, www.salem-news.com/articles/may112010/musical- chairs-dd.php.

21. This well-known quote from John Gardner has been widely circulated.

22. John Piper, *Desiring God* (Sisters, OR: Multnomah, 2011), 302.

23. Belinda Goldsmith, "Is Facebook envy making you miserable?" *NBC News.com,* January 22, 2013.http://nbcnews.to/ila6Y84.

24. Bil Keane, "The Family Circus," comic strip, August 31, 1994.

25. C. S. Lewis, *The Complete C. S. Lewis Signature Classics* (San Francisco: HarperCollins, 2007), 444.

26. Charles Dickens, *A Tale of Two Cities* (Mineola, NY: Dover), 1.

27. Corrie ten Boom and John and Elizabeth Sherrill, *The Hiding Place* (Peabody, MA: Hendrickson, 2006), 55–56.

28. Margaret Clarkson, *So You're Single!* (Wheaton: Harold Shaw, 1978), 21.

29. Jonathan Edwards, *Memoirs of the Rev. David Brainerd: Missionary to the Indians* (New Haven: S. Converse, 1822), 255.

30. Ibid., 31.

31. Martin H. Hanser, *The Westminster Collection of Christian Quotations* (Louisville: Westminster John Knox Press, 2001), 122.

32. Rachel Quillin, *The Christian Quote Book* (Uhrichsville, OH: Barbour), 18.

33. Helen Roseveare, *Give Me This Mountain* (Grand Rapids: Eerdmans, 1966), 150.

34. Ibid., 162.

35. Henrietta Mears, "Henrietta Mears: Biographical Sketch." *Global Adventure*. www.kamglobal.org/BiographicalSketches/henriettamears.html.

36. Billy Graham's introduction in Barbara Hudson Powers, *The Henrietta Mears Story* (Old Tappan, NJ: Revell, 1957), 7.

37. Phyllis Thompson, *A Transparent Woman: The Compelling Story of Gladys Aylward* (Grand Rapids: Zondervan, 1971), 182–83.

38. Ten Boom, Sherrill, and Sherrill, 240.

39. Corrie ten Boom, *Tramp for the Lord: The Story That Begins Where* The Hiding Place *Ends*, (Fort Washington, PA: CLC Publications, 2011), 170.

40. A. Wetherell Johnson, *Created for Commitment* (Carol Stream: Tyndale, 1982), XX.

Acknowledgments

I'm a small-town girl living a big-city life that wouldn't be even possible without the huge posse that has supported me and loved me in the good times and the bad.

First of all I'd like to thank Holly Kisly, who believed in me and convinced me I could write a book one day. She's the best publisher anyone could ever ask for. I'm also thankful for Rene Hanebutt, her partner in crime, who started it all. I'm thankful to Bailey Utecht, my wonderful editor, who sees every single detail and isn't afraid to correct me.

Thank you to the readers of *Living with Power*. You pushed me when I felt like crawling and cheered for me when I felt like no one was watching.

To my church and the women of Harvest Bible Chapel. God has knit my heart with yours and I'm thankful for your patience with me during the early years.

I have to thank Dave Learned, my campus pastor, who gave me the freedom to write when I wanted to.

Thank you to Tina and Sue—friends, leaders, and wise followers of Christ.

To my Friday morning small group: you didn't always hear the full story, but you saw right past my defenses and wormed your way into my heart. Thank you doesn't seem enough.

I'm so thankful for my pastor, James MacDonald, and his wife, Kathy. You have taught me more than you will ever know, and I am forever grateful.

To Lynne. Thank you, my dear, dear friend for sticking by me and listening to me when I was in the pits, and rejoicing with me when I've stood on my little hills of victory.

Renee. I'm not sure I would have had the guts to write this book without you. If I were to sing a Bette Midler song, you'd be the wind beneath my wings. Thank you for praying me through the rough spots. Thank you for waking up with the chickens to keep me on the straight and narrow.

Bonnie. Bonnie. Bonnie. Enough said. No one else could do what you do and still love me. You're the best assistant and mind reader any crazy creative could dream of having. Thank you.

My family. My crazy Lebanese family. I have to name you all or else I won't be able to show my face at Christmas. So here we go: thank you to Nick, Patricia, Maya, Leya, and Fawzi. No one does a holiday better than you do. Thank you to Ramzi for helping me practice what I believe and for teaching me how to pray. Thank you to Rafi, Micah, and Ben. You're a gift to me and a home that I can always run to. Of course Diana is the glue of your home, and she gets a special mention. Diana, you're the best friend and the best sister anyone could ask for. Thank you for decades of counseling me and for nodding exactly when you were supposed to. I think that's at least 50 percent of the reason I am where I am today.

Lastly, my parents. Your pride in me has propelled me and your love for me has protected me. You have kept me grounded and you have exemplified the love of Jesus Christ for me—unconditional and selfless. How could I not succeed with you as my parents?

Lastly—for real this time—I thank Christ Jesus, my Lord and Savior, who has given me life and purpose. He is the friend of this sinner and the Savior of my soul. Your grace has sustained me, and Your love has enthralled me. Please accept this book as an offering of worship to You. Be magnified through me always, or shut me up forever.

GIRLS GONE WISE

978-0-8024-5154-5

Every minute you spend here will help you—or someone you love—replace the emptiness and guilt of being wild with the power of living out God's spectacular design for women.

But be prepared. This isn't your grandmother's handbook on etiquette. It's God's Word powerfully unfolded by someone He's commissioned to speak the truth in love. You'll be captivated, challenged, and impassioned to be far more than the world's model of the perfect woman. You read this book and apply its principles and you'll become something your Heavenly Father and Friend has always intended you to be: *A Girl Gone Wise in a World Gone Wild.*

RADICAL WOMANHOOD

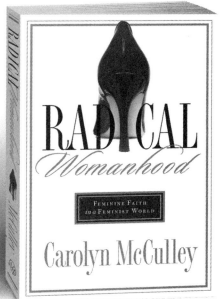

978-0-8024-5084-9

The foundation and core message of *Radical Womanhood* is consistent with the traditional complementarian teaching on biblical womanhood. However, the target audience, tone, and style are radically different. Most books on this subject take a heavily didactic tone that assumes an awareness of Christian lingo and a high degree of spiritual maturity. *Radical Womanhood* has the narrative approach appreciated by postmodern readers, but still incorporates solid, biblically-based teaching for personal application and growth.

Also available as an ebook

MOODY
PUBLISHERS
www.MoodyPublishers.com

I KISSED A LOT OF FROGS

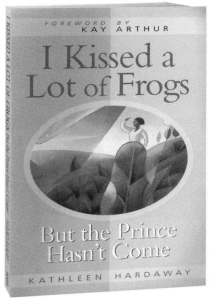

A single's guide for abundant life in Christ

Often singles in the church feel overlooked. Additionally, so many resources are aimed at helping singles prepare for and find mates. Kathleen Hardaway offers *I Kissed A Lot of Frogs* as an indispensable alternative pointing singles to Jesus for their joy, their strength, and their completeness. Sharing her own journey from heartbreak and disappointment to wholeness and contentment, Hardaway helps readers get and stay focused on the perfect plan God has for their lives.

Also available as an ebook

MOODY
PUBLISHERS

www.MoodyPublishers.com